The Kneeling Christian

by the author of
HOW TO LIVE THE VICTORIOUS CHRISTIAN LIFE
An Unknown Christian

Introduction by P.J. ZONDERVAN

ZondervanPublishingHouse
Grand Rapids, Michigan

A Division of HarperCollinsPublishers

THE KNEELING CHRISTIAN
Copyright © 1945, 1971, 1986 by Zondervan Publishing House
Grand Rapids, Michigan

Requests for information should be addressed to:
Zondervan Publishing House
Grand Rapids, Michigan 49530

Library of Congress Cataloging-in-Publication Data

Unknown Christian.
  The kneeling Christian.

  (Clarion classic)
  1. Prayer. I. Title.
BV210.2.U52   1986   248.3'2   86-1542
ISBN 0-310-33491-8 (pbk.)

Printed in the United States of America

      96 97 98 99 00 / DH / 78 77 76 75 74 73

The
Kneeling
Christian

Contents

Introduction

The year was 1937. I was making my first sales trip along the West Coast, representing the Zondervan Publishing House, and I called on a bookseller in Seattle, Washington.

During my conversation with that bookseller I learned of the blessing a book written and published in England had been to her. This was my first introduction to the book *The Kneeling Christian* by an Unknown Christian. The content of the book had been a great blessing to that bookseller.

In view of my interest in the subject of prayer, it didn't take me long to get into this volume. I discovered the author wrote in a simple style, expressing himself concisely and effectively, using understandable illustrations to make the various truths clear and applicable.

It didn't take long for Zondervan to make arrangements with the English publisher to distribute *The Kneeling Christian* to our constituency in America.

Then because of the scarcity of paper and printing equipment in Britain during World War II, the English publisher permitted this valuable and precious book to go out of print.

So we arranged for the rights to print and publish this book in the United States. Since 1945 we have had fifty-six printings (before 1945 no record was maintained of the number of printings) with a circulation of more than 400,000 copies in print.

Now it's a privilege to make this classic work on prayer available in the handy and popular trade paperback size in Zondervan's Clarion Classics series. I pray that this volume will be a blessing to every reader as it has been a blessing to me and thousands of others around the world.

P.J. ZONDERVAN

Author's Preface

A traveler in China visited a heathen temple on a great feast day. Many were the worshipers of the hideous idol enclosed in a sacred shrine. The visitor noticed that most of the devotees brought with them small pieces of paper on which prayers had been written or printed. These were wrapped up in little balls of stiff mud and flung at the idol. He enquired the reason for this strange proceeding and was told that if the mud ball stuck fast to the idol, then the prayer would assuredly be answered; but if the mud fell off, the prayer was rejected by the god.

We may smile at this peculiar way of testing the acceptability of prayer. But is it not a fact that the majority of Christian men and women who pray to a Living God know very little about real prevailing prayer? Yet prayer is the key that unlocks the door of God's treasure-house.

It is not too much to say that all real growth in the spiritual life—all victory over temptation, all confidence and peace in the presence of difficulties and dangers, all repose of spirit in times of great disappointment or loss, all habitual communion with God—depends upon the practice of secret prayer.

This book was written by request and with much hesitancy. It goes forth with much prayer. May He Who said, "Men ought always to pray, and not to faint," "teach us to pray."

The
Kneeling
Christian

Chapter 1

God's Great Need

"God wondered." This is a very striking thought! The very boldness of the idea ought surely to arrest the attention of every earnest Christian man, woman, and child. A wondering God! Why, how staggered we might well be if we knew the cause of God's "wonder"! Yet we will find it to be, apparently, a very little thing. But if we are willing to consider the matter carefully, we shall discover it to be one of the greatest possible importance to everyone who believes on the Lord Jesus Christ. Nothing else is so momentous or so vital to our spiritual welfare.

God "wondered that here was no intercessor" (Isa. 59:16), "none to interpose" (RV marg.). But this was in the days of long ago, before the coming of the Lord Jesus Christ "full of grace and truth"; before the outpouring of the Holy Spirit, full of grace and power, "helping our infirmity," "Himself making intercession for us" and in us (Rom. 8:26). Yes, and before the truly amazing promises of our Savior regarding prayer and before men knew very much about prayer; in the days when sacrifices for their sins loomed larger in their eyes than supplication for other sinners.

Oh, how great must be God's wonder today! For how few there are among us who know what prevailing prayer really is! Every one of us would confess that we believe in prayer, yet how many of us truly believe in the power of prayer? Now, before we go a step farther, may the writer most earnestly implore you not to read hurriedly what is contained in these chapters. Much—very much—depends upon the way in which every reader receives what is here recorded. For everything depends upon prayer.

Why are many Christians so often defeated? Because they pray so little. Why are many church-workers so often discouraged and disheartened? Because they pray so little.

Why do most men see so few brought "out of darkness to light" by their ministry? Because they pray so little.

Why are not our churches simply on fire for God? Because there is so little real prayer.

The Lord Jesus is as powerful today as ever before. The Lord Jesus is as anxious for men to be saved as ever before. His arm is not shortened that it cannot save, but He cannot stretch forth His arm unless we pray more—and more.

We may be assured of this: the secret of all failure is our failure in secret prayer.

If God "wondered" in the days of Isaiah, we need not be surprised to find that in the days of His flesh our Lord "marveled." He marveled at the unbelief of some, unbelief that actually prevented Him from doing any mighty work in their cities (Mark 6:6).

But we must remember that those who were guilty of this unbelief saw no beauty in Him that they should desire Him or believe on Him. What then must His "marvel" be today, when He sees amongst us so few who do truly love and adore Him, so few who really "stir themselves up to take hold of God" (Isa. 64:7). Surely there is nothing so absolutely astonishing as a practically prayerless Christian? These are eventful and ominous days. In fact, there are many evidences that these are "the last days" in which God promised to pour out His Spirit—the Spirit of supplication—upon all flesh (Joel 2:28). Yet the vast majority of professing Christians scarcely know what "supplication" means. Many of our churches not only have no prayer meetings but sometimes unblushingly condemn such meetings and even ridicule them.

The Church of England, recognizing the importance of worship and prayer, expects her clergy to read prayers in Church every morning and evening.

But when this is done, is it not often in an empty church? And are not the prayers frequently raced through at a pace that precludes real worship? "Common prayer," too, often must necessarily be rather vague and indefinite.

And what of those churches where the old-fashioned weekly prayer meeting is retained? Would not "weakly" be the more appropriate word? C. H. Spurgeon had the joy of being able to say that he conducted a prayer meeting every Monday night "which scarcely ever numbers less than from a thousand to twelve hundred attendants."

My brothers, have we ceased to believe in prayer? If you still hold your weekly gathering for prayer, is it not a fact that the very great majority of your church members never come near it? Yes, and never even think of coming near it. Why is this? Whose fault is it?

"Only a prayer meeting"! How often we have heard the utterance! How many of those reading these words really enjoy a prayer meeting? Is it a joy or just a duty? Please forgive me for asking so many questions and for pointing out what appears to be a perilous weakness and a lamentable shortcoming in our churches. We are not out to criticize, far less to condemn. Anybody can do that. Our yearning desire is to stir up Christians "to take hold of" God as never before. We wish to encourage, to enhearten, to uplift.

We are never so high as when we are on our knees.

Criticize? Who dares criticize another? When one looks back upon the past and remembers how much prayerlessness there has been in one's own life, words of criticism of others wither away on the lips.

But we believe the time has come when a clarion call to the individual and to the Church is needed, a call to prayer.

Now, dare we face this question of prayer? It seems a foolish query, for is not prayer a part and parcel of all religions? Yet we venture to ask our readers to look at this matter fairly and squarely. Do I really believe that prayer is a power? Is prayer the greatest power on earth, or is it not? Does prayer indeed "move the Hand that moves the world"?

Do God's prayer commands really concern Me? Do the promises of God concerning prayer still hold good? We have all been muttering, "Yes, yes, yes," as we read these questions. We dare not say "No" to any one of them. And yet . . .

Has it ever occurred to you that our Lord never gave an unnecessary or an optional command? Do we really believe that our Lord never made a promise that He could not or would not fulfill? Our Savior's three great commands for definite action were:

> Pray ye—
> Do this—
> Go ye!

Are we obeying Him? How often His command, "Do this," is reiterated by our preachers today! One might almost think it was His only command! How seldom we are reminded of His bidding to "pray" and to "go." Yet without obedience to the "pray ye," it is of little or no use at all either to "do this" or to "go."

In fact, it can easily be shown that all want of success (and all failure in the spiritual life and in Christian work) is due to defective or insufficient prayer. Unless we pray aright we cannot live aright or serve aright. This may appear, at first sight, to be gross exaggeration, but the more we think it over in the light Scripture throws upon it, the more convinced shall we be of the truth of this statement.

Now, as we begin once more to see what the Bible has to say about this mysterious and wonderful subject, shall we endeavor to read some of our Lord's promises as though we had never heard them before. What will the effect be?

Some twenty years ago the writer was studying in a Theological College. One morning, early, a fellow student, who is today one of England's foremost missionaries, burst into the room holding an open Bible in his hands. Although he was preparing for Holy Orders, he was at that time only a young convert to Christ.

He had gone up to the University "caring for none of these things." Popular, clever, athletic, he had already won a place amongst the smart set of his college when Christ claimed him. He accepted the Lord Jesus as a personal Savior and became a very keen follower of his Master. The Bible was, comparatively, a new book to him, and as a result he was constantly making "discoveries."

On that memorable day on which he invaded my quietude, he cried excitedly, his face all aglow with mingled joy and surprise, "Do you believe this? Is it really true?"

"Believe what?" I asked, glancing at the open Bible with some astonishment.

"Why this . . ." and he read in eager tones St. Matthew 21:21–22: " 'If ye have faith and doubt not . . . all things whatsoever ye shall ask in prayer, believing, ye shall receive.' Do you believe it? Is it true?"

"Yes," I replied, with much surprise at his excitement, "of course it's true; of course I believe it."

Yet through my mind there flashed all manner of thoughts! "Well, that's a very wonderful promise," said he. "It seems to me to be absolutely limitless! Why don't we pray more?"

And he went away, leaving me thinking hard.

I had never looked at those verses quite in that way. As the door closed upon that eager young follower of the Master, I had a vision of my Savior and His love and His power such as I never had before. I had a vision of a life of prayer, yes, and "limitless" power, which I saw depended upon two things only: faith and prayer.

For the moment I was thrilled. I fell on my knees, and as I bowed before my Lord what thoughts surged through my mind, what hopes and aspirations flooded my soul! God was speaking to me in an extraordinary way. This was a great call to prayer. But—to my shame be it said—I heeded not that call.

Where did I fail? True, I prayed a little more than before, but nothing much seemed to happen. Why? Was it because I did not see what a high standard the Savior requires in the inner life of those who would pray successfully?

Was it because I had failed to measure up my life to the "perfect love" standard so beautifully described in the thirteenth chapter of the first Epistle to the Corinthians?

For, after all, prayer is not just putting into action good

resolutions "to pray." Like David, we need to cry, "Create in me a clean heart, O God" (Ps. 51) before we can pray aright. And the inspired words of the Apostle of Love need to be heeded today as much as ever before: "Beloved, if our heart condemn us not, we have boldness toward God; and [then] whatsoever we ask, we receive of Him" (1 John 3:21—22).

"True. And I believe it." Yes, indeed, it is a limitless promise, and yet how little we realize it, how little we claim from Christ. And our Lord "marvels" at our unbelief. But if we could only read the Gospels for the first time, what an amazing book it would seem! Should we not "marvel" and "wonder"? And today I pass on that great call to you. Will you give heed to it? Will you profit by it? Or shall it fall on deaf ears and leave you prayerless?

Fellow Christians, let us awake! The Devil is blinding our eyes. He is endeavoring to prevent us from facing this question of prayer.

These pages are written by special request. But it is many months since that request came. Every attempt to begin to write has been frustrated, and even now one is conscious of a strange reluctance to do so. There seems to be some mysterious power restraining the hand. Do we realize that there is nothing the Devil dreads so much as prayer? His great concern is to keep us from praying. He loves to see us "up to our eyes" in work, provided we do not pray. He does not fear because we are eager and earnest Bible students, provided we are little in prayer.

Someone has wisely said, "Satan laughs at our toiling, mocks at our wisdom, but trembles when we pray." All this is so familiar to us, but do we really pray? If not, then failure must dog our footsteps whatever signs of apparent success there may be.

Let us never forget that the greatest thing we can do for God or for man is to pray. For we can accomplish far more by our prayers than by our work.

Prayer is omnipotent; it can do anything that God can do! When we pray God works. All fruitfulness in service is the outcome of prayer, of the worker's prayers, or of those who are holding up holy hands on his behalf.

We all know how to pray, but perhaps many of us need to cry as the disciples did of old, "Lord, teach us to pray."

O Lord, by Whom we come to God,
The Life, the Truth, the Way,
The path of prayer Thyself hast trod;
Lord, teach us now to pray.

Chapter 2

Almost Incredible Promises

"When we stand with Christ in glory, looking o'er life's finished story," the most amazing feature of that life as it is looked back upon will be its prayerlessness.

We shall be almost beside ourselves with astonishment that we spent so little time in real intercession. It will be our turn to "wonder."

In our Lord's last discourse to His loved ones, just before the most wonderful of all prayers, the Master again and again held out His kingly golden scepter and said, as it were, "What is your request? It shall be granted unto you, even unto the whole of My kingdom!"

Do we believe this? We must do so if we believe our Bibles. Shall we just read over very quietly and thoughtfully one of our Lord's promises, reiterated so many times? If we had never read them before, we should open our eyes in bewilderment, for these promises are almost incredible. From the lips of any mere man they would be quite unbelievable. But it is the Lord of heaven and earth Who speaks, and He is speaking at the most solemn moment of His life. It is the eve of His death and passion. It is a farewell message. Now listen!

"Verily, verily I say unto you, he that believeth on Me, the works that I do shall he do also; and greater works than these shall he do; because I go unto the Father. And whatsoever ye shall ask in My name, that will I do, that the

Father may be glorified in the Son. If ye shall ask me anything in My name, that will I do" (John 14:12–14). Now, could any words be plainer or clearer than these? Could any promise be greater or grander? Has anyone else, anywhere, at any time, ever offered so much?

How staggered those disciples must have been! Surely they could scarcely believe their own ears. But that promise is made also to you and to me.

And, lest there should be any mistake on their part or on ours, our Lord repeats Himself a few moments afterward. Yes, and the Holy Spirit bids St. John record those words again: "If ye abide in Me, and My words abide in you, ask whatsoever ye will, and it shall be done unto you. Herein is My Father glorified, that ye bear much fruit; and so shall ye be My disciples" (John 15:7–8).

These words are of such grave importance and so momentous that the Savior of the world is not content even with a threefold utterance of them. He urges His disciples to obey His command "to ask." In fact, He tells them that one sign of their being His "friends" will be the obedience to His commands in all things (v. 14). Then He once more repeats His wishes: "Ye did not choose Me, but I chose you, and appointed you, that ye should go and bear fruit, and that your fruit should abide: that whatsoever ye shall ask of the Father in My name, He may give it you" (John 15:16).

One would think that our Lord had now made it plain enough that He wanted them to pray; that He needed their prayers and that without prayer they could accomplish nothing. But to our intense surprise He returns again to the same subject, saying very much the same words.

"In that day ye shall ask Me nothing"—*i.e.*, "ask Me no question" (RV marg.)—"Verily, verily I say unto you, if ye shall ask anything of the Father, He will give it you in My name. Hitherto have ye asked nothing in My name: ask, and ye shall receive, that your joy may be fulfilled" (John 16:23–24).

Never before had our Lord laid such stress on any promise or command—never! This truly marvelous promise is given us six times over. Six times, almost in the same breath, our

Savior commands us to ask whatsoever we will. This is the greatest, the most wonderful promise ever made to man. Yet most people—Christian people—practically ignore it! Is it not so?

The exceeding greatness of the promise seems to overwhelm us. Yet we know that He is "able to do exceeding abundantly above all that we ask or think" (Eph. 3:20).

So our blessed Master gives the final exhortation before He is seized, bound, and scourged, before His gracious lips are silenced on the cross: "Ye shall ask in My name . . . for the Father Himself loveth you" (John 16:26–27). We have often spent much time in reflecting upon our Lord's seven words from the cross. And it is well we should do so. Have we ever spent one hour in meditating upon this, our Savior's sevenfold invitation to pray?

Today He sits on the throne of His Majesty on high, and He holds out to us the scepter of His power. Shall we touch it and tell Him our desires? He bids us take of His treasures. He yearns to grant us "according to the riches of His glory," that we may "be strengthened with power through His Spirit in the inner man." He tells us that our strength and our fruitfulness depend upon our prayers. He reminds us that our very joy depends upon answered prayer (John 16:24).

And yet we allow the Devil to persuade us to neglect prayer! He makes us believe that we can do more by our own efforts than by our prayers, more by our intercourse with men than by our intercession with God. It passes one's comprehension that so little heed should be given to our Lord's sevenfold invitation, command, promise! How dare we work for Christ without being much on our knees? Quite recently an earnest Christian "worker," a Sunday school teacher and communicant, wrote me: "I have never had an answer to prayer in all my life." But why? Is God a liar? Is not God trustworthy? Do His promises count for naught? Does He not mean what He says? And doubtless there are many reading these words who in their hearts are saying the same thing as that Christian worker. Payson is right, is scriptural, when he says: "If we would do much for God, we must ask much of God: we must be men of prayer." If our prayers are not answered—always answered but not necessarily granted—the fault must be entirely in ourselves and not in God. God delights to answer prayer, and He has given us His word that He will answer.

Fellow laborers in His vineyard, it is quite evident that our Master desires us to ask and to ask much. He tells us we glorify God by doing so! Nothing is beyond the scope of prayer that is not beyond the will of God, and we do not desire to go beyond His will.

We dare not say that our Lord's words are not true. Yet somehow or other few Christians really seem to believe them. What holds us back? What seals our lips? What keeps us from making much of prayer? Do we doubt His love? Never! He gave His life for us and to us. Do we doubt the Father's love? Nay. "The Father Himself loveth you," said Christ when urging His disciples to pray.

Do we doubt His power? Not for a moment. Hath He not said, "All power hath been given unto Me in heaven and on earth. Go ye . . . and lo, I am with you always . . ." (Matt. 28:18–20)? Do we doubt His wisdom? Do we mistrust His choice for us? Not for a moment. And yet so very few of His followers consider prayer really worthwhile. Of course, they would deny this, but actions speak louder than words. Are we afraid to put God to the test? He has said we may do so. "Bring Me the whole tithe into the storehouse . . . and prove Me now herewith, saith the Lord of Hosts, if I will not open you the windows of heaven, and pour you out a blessing that there shall not be room enough to receive it" (Mal. 3:10). Whenever God makes us a promise, let us boldly say, as did St. Paul, "I believe God" (Acts 27:25), and trust Him to keep His word.

Shall we begin today to be men of prayer, if we have never done so before? Let us not put if off till a more convenient season. God wants me to pray. The dear Savior wants me to pray. He needs my prayers. So much—in fact, everything—depends upon prayer. How dare we hold back? Let every one of us ask on our knees this question: "If no one on earth prayed for the salvation of sinners more fervently or more frequently than I do, how many of them would be converted to God through prayer?"

Do we spend ten minutes a day in prayer? Do we consider it important enough for that?

Ten minutes a day on our knees in prayer—when the Kingdom of Heaven can be had for the asking!

Ten minutes? It seems a very inadequate portion of our time to spend in taking hold of God (Isa. 64:7)!

And is it prayer when we do "say" our prayers, or are we just repeating daily a few phrases that have become practically meaningless while our thoughts are wandering hither and thither?

If God were to answer the words we repeated on our knees this morning should we know it? Should we recognize the answer? Do we even remember what we asked for? He does answer. He has given us His word for it. He always answers every real prayer of faith.

But we shall see what the Bible has to say on this point in a later chapter. We are now thinking of the amount of time we spend in prayer.

"How often do you pray?" was the question put to a Christian woman. "Three times a day, and all the day beside," was the quick reply. But how many are there like that? Is prayer to me just a duty, or is it a privilege, a pleasure, a real joy, a necessity?

Let us get a fresh vision of Christ in all His glory and a fresh glimpse of all the "riches of His glory" that He places at our disposal and of all the mighty power given unto Him. Then let us get a fresh vision of the world and all its needs. (And the world was never so needy as it is today.)

Why, the wonder is not that we pray so little but that we can ever get up from our knees if we realize our own need; the needs of our home and our loved ones; the needs of our pastor and the Church; the needs of our city, of our country, of the heathen and Mohammedan world! All these needs can be met by the riches of God in Christ Jesus. St. Paul had no doubt about this; nor have we. Yes! "My God shall supply all your need according to His riches in glory by Christ Jesus" (Phil. 4:19). But to share His riches we must pray, for the same Lord is rich unto all that call upon Him (Rom. 10:12).

So great is the importance of prayer that God has taken care to anticipate all the excuses or objections we may be likely to make.

People plead their weakness or infirmity, or they declare they do not know how to pray.

God foresaw this inability long ages ago. Did He not inspire St. Paul to say: "The Spirit also helpeth our infirmity: for we know not how to pray as we ought; but the Spirit Himself maketh intercession for us with groanings that cannot be uttered; and He that searcheth the hearts knoweth what is the mind of the Spirit, because He maketh intercession for the saints according to the will of God" (Rom. 8:26–27)?

Yes. Every provision is made for us. But only the Holy Spirit can "stir us up" to "take hold of God." And if we will but yield ourselves to the Spirit's promptings we shall most assuredly follow the example of the apostles of old, who "gave themselves to prayer" and "continued steadfastly in prayer" (Acts 6:4 RV).

We may rest fully assured of this: a man's influence in the world can be gauged not by his eloquence or his zeal or his orthodoxy or his energy but by his prayers. Yes, and we will go farther and maintain that no man can live aright who does not pray aright.

We may work for Christ from morn till night; we may spend much time in Bible study; we may be most earnest and faithful and "acceptable" in our preaching and in our individual dealing, but none of these things can be truly effective unless we are much in prayer. We shall only be full of good works and not "bearing fruit in every good work" (Col. 1:10). To be little with God in prayer is to be little for God in service. Much secret prayer means much public power. Yet is it not a fact that while our organizing is nearly perfect, our agonizing in prayer is well nigh lost?

Men are wondering why the Revival delays its coming. There is only one thing that can delay it, and that is lack of prayer. All Revivals have been the outcome of prayer. One sometimes longs for the voice of an archangel, but what would that avail if the voice of Christ Himself does not stir us up to pray? It seems almost impertinence for any man to take up the cry when our Savior has put forth His "limitless" promises. Yet we feel that something should be done, and we believe that the Holy Spirit is prompting men to remind themselves and others of Christ's words and power. No words of mine can impress men with the value of prayer, the need of prayer, and the omnipotence of prayer.

But these utterances go forth steeped in prayer that God the Holy Spirit will Himself convict Christian men and women of the sin of prayerlessness and drive them to their knees, to call upon God day and night in burning, believing, prevailing intercession! The Lord Jesus, now in the heavenlies, beckons to us to fall upon our knees and claim the riches of His grace.

No man dare prescribe for another how long a time he ought to spend in prayer, nor do we suggest that men should make a vow to pray so many minutes or hours a day. Of course, the Bible's command is to "Pray without ceasing." This is evidently the "attitude of prayer"—the attitude of one's life.

Here we are speaking of definite acts of prayer. Have you ever timed your prayers? We believe that most of our readers would be amazed and confounded if they did time themselves!

Some years ago the writer faced this prayer question. He felt that for himself at least one hour a day was the minimum time that he should spend in prayer. He carefully noted down every day a record of his prayer life. As time went on he met a working man who was being much used of God.

When asked to what he chiefly attributed his success, this man quietly replied, "Well, I could not get on without two hours a day of private prayer."

Then there came across my path a Spirit-filled missionary from overseas, who told very humbly of the wonderful things God was doing through his ministry. (One could see all along that God was given all the praise and all the glory.) "I find it necessary, oftentimes, to spend four hours a day in prayer," said this missionary.

And we remember how the Greatest Missionary of all sometimes used to spend whole nights in prayer. Why? Our blessed Lord did not pray simply as an example to us; He never did things merely as an example. He prayed because He needed to pray. As perfect Man, prayer to Him was a necessity. Then how much more is it necessary to you and me?

"Four hours a day in prayer!" exclaimed a man who is giving his whole life to Christian work as a medical missionary. "Four hours? Give me ten minutes and I'm done!" That was an honest and a brave confession, even if a sad one. Yet if some of us were to speak out as honestly . . . ?

Now, it was not by accident that these men crossed my path. God was speaking through them. It was just another "call to prayer" from the "God of patience," who is also a "God of comfort" (Rom. 15:5), and when their quiet message had sunk into my soul a book came into my hands "by chance," as people say. It told briefly and simply the story of John Hyde—"Praying Hyde," as he came to be called. Just as God sent St. John the Baptist to prepare the way of our Lord at His first coming, so He sent in these last days St. John the Pray-er, to make straight paths for His coming again. "Praying Hyde"—what a name! As one read of this marvelous life of prayer, one began to ask, "Have I ever prayed?"

I found others were asking the same question. One lady, who is noted for her wonderful intercession, wrote me, saying, "When I laid down this book, I began to think I had never in all my life really prayed!"

But here we must leave the matter. Shall we get on our knees before God and allow His Holy Spirit to search us through and through? Are we sincere? Do we really desire to do God's will? Do we really believe His promises? If so, will it not lead us to spend more time on our knees before God? Do not vow to pray "so much" a day. Resolve to pray much, but prayer, to be of value, must be spontaneous and not from constraint.

But we must bear in mind that mere resolutions to take

more time for prayer and to conquer reluctance to pray will not prove lastingly effective unless there is a wholehearted and absolute surrender to the Lord Jesus Christ. If we have never taken this step, we must take it now if we desire to be people of prayer.

I am quite certain of this fact: God wants me to pray, wants you to pray. The question is, are we willing to pray?

Gracious Savior, pour out upon us the fullness of the Holy Spirit that we may indeed become Kneeling Christians.

> To God your every want
> In instant prayer display.
> Pray always; pray and never faint:
> Pray! Without ceasing, pray.

Chapter 3

"Ask of Me and I Will Give"

God wants me to pray, to be much in prayer because all success in spiritual work is dependent on prayer.

A preacher who prays little may see some results of his labors, but if he does it will be because someone somewhere is praying for him. The "fruit" is the prayer's, not the preacher's. How surprised some of us preachers will be on that day when the Lord shall "reward every man according to his works." "Lord! Those were my converts! It was I who conducted that mission at which so many were brought into the fold." Ah, yes, I did the preaching, the pleading, the persuading; but was it "I" who did the praying?

Every convert is the result of the Holy Spirit's pleading in answer to the prayers of some believer.

O God, grant that such surprise may not be ours. O Lord, teach us to pray!

We have had a vision of a God pleadingly calling for prayer from His children. How am I treating that call? Can I say with St. Paul, "I am 'not disobedient to the heavenly vision'"? Again we repeat, if there are any regrets in heaven, the greatest will be that we spent so little time in real intercession while we were on earth.

Think of the wide sweep of prayer! "Ask of Me, and I will give thee the heathen for thine inheritance, and the uttermost parts of the earth for thy possession" (Ps. 2:8). Yet many people do not trouble to bring even the little details of their own lives to God in prayer, and nine out of ten Christian people never think of praying for the heathen!

One is staggered at the unwillingness of Christians to pray. Perhaps it is because they have never experienced or even heard of convincing answers to prayer.

In this chapter we are setting out to do the "impossible." What is that? We long to bring home to the heart and conscience of every reader the power of prayer. We venture to describe this as "impossible." For if men will not believe and act upon our Lord's promises and commands, how can we expect them to be persuaded by any mere human exhortations?

But do you remember that our Lord, when speaking to His disciples, asked them to believe that He was in the Father and the Father in Him? Then He added: If you cannot believe My bare word about this, "believe Me for the very works' sake" (John 14:11). It was as if He said, "If My Person, My sanctified life, and My wonderful words do not elicit belief in Me, then look at My works: surely they are sufficient to compel belief? Believe Me because of what I do."

Then He went on to promise that if they would believe, they should do greater works than these. It was after this utterance that He gave the first of those six wonderful promises in regard to prayer. The inference surely is that those "greater works" are to be done only as the outcome of prayer.

May the disciple therefore follow the Master's method? Fellow worker, if you fail to grasp, fail to trust our Lord's astounding promises regarding prayer, will you not believe them "for the very works' sake"? That is, because of those "greater works" that men and women are performing today, or rather, the works that the Lord Jesus is doing through their prayerful cooperation?

What are we "out for"? What is our real aim in life? Surely we desire most of all to be abundantly fruitful in the Master's service. We seek not position or prominence or power. But we do long to be fruitful servants. Then we must be much in prayer. God can do more through our prayers than through our preaching. A. J. Gordon once said, "You can do more than pray, after you have prayed, but you can never do more than pray until you have prayed." If only we would believe this!

A lady in India was cast down through the failure of her life and work. She was a devoted missionary, but somehow or other conversions never resulted from her ministry.

The Holy Spirit seemed to say to her, "Pray more." But she resisted the promptings of the Spirit for some time. "At length," she said, "I set apart much of my time for prayer. I did it in fear and trembling lest my fellow workers should complain that I was shirking my work. After a few weeks I began to see men and women accepting Christ as their Savior. Moreover, the whole district was soon awakened, and the work of all the other missionaries was blessed as never before. God did more in six months than I had succeeded in doing in six years. And," she added, "no one ever accused me of shirking my duty." Another missionary in India felt the same call to pray. She began to give much time to prayer. No opposition came from without, but it did come from within. But she persisted, and in two years the baptized converts increased sixfold!

God promised that He would "pour out the Spirit of grace and supplication upon all flesh" (Joel 2:28). How much of that Spirit of "supplication" is ours? Surely we must get that Spirit at all costs? Yet if we are not willing to spend time in "supplication," God must perforce withhold His Spirit, and we become numbered among those who are "resisting the Spirit" and possibly "quenching" the Spirit. Has not our Lord promised the Holy Spirit to them that ask (Luke 11:13)?

Are not the very converts from heathendom putting some of us to shame?

A few years ago, when in India, I had the great joy of seeing something of Pandita Ramabai's work. She had a boarding school of 1,500 Hindu girls. One day some of these girls came with their Bibles and asked a missionary what St. Luke 12:49 meant: "I came to cast fire upon the earth; and what will I, if it is already kindled?" The missionary tried to put them off with an evasive answer, not being very sure herself what those words meant. But they were not satisfied, so they determined to pray for this fire. And as they prayed, and because they prayed, the fire of heaven came into their souls. A very Pentecost from above was granted them. No wonder they continued to pray!

A party of these girls upon whom God had poured the "Spirit of supplication" came to a mission house where I spent some weeks. "May we stay here in your town and pray for your work?" they asked. The missionary did not entertain the idea with any great enthusiasm. He felt that they ought to be at school and not "gadding about" the country. But they only asked for a hall or barn where they could pray, and we all value prayers on our behalf. So their request was granted, and the good man sat down to his evening meal, thinking. As the evening wore on, a native pastor came round. He broke down completely. He explained, with tears running down his face, that God's Holy Spirit had convicted him of sin and that he felt compelled to come and openly confess his wrongdoing. He was quickly followed by one Christian after another, all under deep conviction of sin.

There was a remarkable time of blessing. Backsliders were restored, believers were sanctified, and heathen brought into the fold—all because a few mere children were praying.

God is no respecter of persons. If anyone is willing to conform to His conditions, He for His part will assuredly fulfill His promises. Does not our heart burn within us as we hear of God's wonderful power? And that power is ours for the asking. I know there are "conditions." But you and I can fulfill them all through Christ. And those of us who cannot have the privilege of serving God in India or any other overseas mission may yet take our part in bringing down a like blessing. When the Revival in Wales was at its height, a Welsh missionary wrote home begging the people to pray that India might be moved in like manner. So the coal miners met daily at the pit-mouth half an hour before dawn to pray for their comrades overseas. In a few weeks' time the welcome message was sent home: "The blessing has come."

Isn't it just splendid to know that by our prayers we can bring down showers of blessing upon India or Africa or

China just as readily as we can get the few drops needed for our own little plot?

Many of us will recall the wonderful things that God did for Korea a few years ago, entirely in answer to prayer. A few missionaries decided to meet together to pray daily at noon. At the end of the month one brother proposed that, "as nothing had happened," the prayer meeting should be discontinued. "Let us each pray at home as we find it convenient," said he. The others, however, protested that they ought rather to spend even more time in prayer each day. So they continued the daily prayer meeting for four months. Then suddenly the blessing began to be poured out. Church services here and there were interrupted by weeping and confessing of sins. At length a mighty revival broke out. At one place during a Sunday evening service the leading man in the church stood up and confessed that he had stolen one hundred dollars in administering a widow's legacy. Immediately conviction of sin swept the audience. That service did not end till 2 o'clock on Monday morning. God's wondrous power was felt as never before. And when the Church was purified, many sinners found salvation.

Multitudes flocked to the churches out of curiosity. Some came to mock, but fear laid hold of them, and they stayed to pray. Among the "curious" was a brigand chief, the leader of a robber band. He was convicted and converted. He went straight off to the magistrate and gave himself up. "You have no accuser," said the astonished official, "yet you accuse yourself! We have no law in Korea to meet your case." So he dismissed him.

One of the missionaries declared, "It paid well to have spent several months in prayer, for when God gave the Holy Spirit, He accomplished more in half a day than all the missionaries together could have accomplished in half a year." In less than two months, more than 2,000 heathens were converted. The burning zeal of those converts has become a byword. Some of them gave all they had to build a church and wept because they could not give more. Needless to say, they realized the power of prayer. Those converts were themselves baptized with the "Spirit of supplication."

In one church it was announced that a daily prayer meeting would be held at 4:30 every morning. The very first day 400 people arrived long before the stated hour—eager to pray! The number rapidly increased to 600 as days went on. At Seoul, 1,100 is the average attendance at the weekly prayer meeting.

Heathen people came to see what was happening. They exclaimed in astonishment, "The living God is among you." Those poor heathen saw what many Christians fail to see. Did not Christ say, "Where two or three are gathered together in My name, there am I in the midst of them" (Matt. 18:20)? What is possible in Korea is possible here. God is "no respecter" of nations. He is longing to bless us, longing to pour His Spirit upon us.

Now if we here in this so-called Christian country really believed in prayer, *i.e.*, in our Lord's own gracious promises, should we avoid prayer meetings? If we had any genuine concern for the lost condition of thousands in our own land and tens of thousands in heathen lands, should we withhold our prayers? Surely we do not think, or we would pray more. "Ask of Me—I will give," says an almighty, all-loving God, and we scarcely heed His words!

Verily, converts from heathendom put us to shame. In my journeyings I came to Rawal Pindi, in northwest India. What do you think happened there? Some of Pandita Ramabai's girls went there to camp. But a little while before this, Pandita Ramabai had said to her girls, "If there is any blessing in India, we may have it. Let us ask God to tell us what we must do in order to have the blessing."

As she read her Bible she paused over the verses, "Wait for the promise of the Father . . . ye shall receive power after that the Holy Ghost is come upon you" (Acts 1:4–8). "Wait! Why, we have never done this," she cried. "We have prayed, but we have never expected any greater blessing today than we had yesterday!" Oh, how they prayed! One prayer meeting lasted six hours. And what a marvelous blessing God poured out in answer to their prayers.

While some of these girls were at Rawal Pindi, a missionary, looking out of her tent toward midnight, was surprised to see a light burning in one of the girls' tents, a thing quite contrary to rules. She went to expostulate but found the youngest of those ten girls, a child of fifteen, kneeling in the farthest corner of the tent, holding a little tallow candle in one hand and a list of names for intercession in the other. She had 500 names on her list, 500 out of the 1,500 girls in Pandita Ramabai's school. Hour after hour she was naming them before God. No wonder God's blessing fell wherever those girls went and upon whoever those girls prayed for.

Pastor Ding Li Mei of China has the names of 1,100 students on his prayer list. Many hundreds have been won to Christ through his prayers. And so out-and-out are his converts that many scores of them have entered the Christian ministry.

It would be an easy matter to add to these amazing and inspiring stories of blessing through prayer. But there is no need to do so. I know that God wants me to pray. I know that God wants you to pray.

"If there is any blessing in England we may have it." Nay, more: if there is any blessing in Christ, we may have it. "Blessed be the God and Father of our Lord Jesus Christ, who hath blessed us with every spiritual blessing in the heavenly places in Christ" (Eph. 1:3). God's great storehouse is full of blessings. Only prayer can unlock that storehouse. Prayer is the key, and faith turns the key and opens the door and claims the blessing. Blessed are the pure in heart, for they shall see God. And to see Him is to pray aright.

Listen! We have come, you and I, once more to the parting of the ways. All our past failure, all our past inefficiency and insufficiency, all our past unfruitfulness in service, can be banished now, once and for all, if we only give prayer its proper place. Do it today. Do not wait for a more convenient time.

Everything worth having depends upon the decision we make. Truly God is a wonderful God! And one of the most wonderful things about Him is that He puts His all at the disposal of the prayer of faith. Believing prayer from a wholly-cleansed heart never fails. God has given us His word for it. Yet vastly more wonderful is the amazing fact that Christian men and women should either not believe God's word or should fail to put it to the test.

When Christ is "all in all," when He is Savior and Lord and King of our whole being, then it is really He Who prays our prayers. We can then truthfully alter one word of a well-known verse and say that the Lord Jesus ever liveth to make intercession in us. Oh, that we might make the Lord Jesus "marvel" not at our unbelief but at our faith! When our Lord shall again "marvel" and say of us, "Verily . . . I have not found so great faith, no, not in Israel" (Matt. 8:10), then indeed shall "palsy" (paralysis) be transformed into power.

Has not our Lord come to "cast fire" upon us? Are we "already kindled"? Can He not use us as much as He used those mere children of Khedgaon? God is no respecter of persons. If we can humbly and truthfully say, "To me to live is Christ" (Phil. 1:21), will He not manifest forth His mighty power in us?

Some of us have been reading about Praying Hyde. Truly, his intercession changed things. People tell us that they were thrilled when John Hyde prayed. They were stirred to their inmost being when he just pleaded the name "Jesus! Jesus! Jesus!" and a baptism of love and power came upon them.

But it was not John Hyde, it was the Holy Spirit of God whom one consecrated man, filled with that Spirit, brought down upon all around him. May we not all become "Praying Hydes"? Do you say, "No, he had a special gift of prayer"? Very well, how did he get it? He was once an ordinary Christian man, just like any of us.

Have you noticed that, humanly speaking, he owed his prayer life to the prayers of his father's friend? Now get hold of this point. It is one of greatest importance and one that may profoundly affect your whole life. Perhaps I may be allowed to tell the story fully, for so much depends upon it. Shall we quote John Hyde himself? He was on board a ship sailing for India, whither he was going as a missionary. He says, "My father had a friend who greatly desired to be a foreign missionary but was not permitted to go. This friend wrote me a letter directed in care of the ship. I received it a few hours out of New York harbor. The words were not many, but the purpose of them was this: 'I shall not cease praying for you, dear John, until you are filled with the Holy Spirit.' When I had read the letter I crumpled it up in anger and threw it on the deck. Did this friend think I had not received the baptism of the Spirit or that I would think of going to India without this equipment? I was angry. But by and by better judgment prevailed, and I picked up the letter and read it again. Possibly I did need something that I had not yet received. I paced up and down the deck, a battle raging within. I felt uncomfortable: I loved the writer; I knew the holy life he lived, and down in my heart there was a conviction that he was right, and that I was not fit to be a missionary. . . . This went on for two or three days, until I felt perfectly miserable. . . . At last, in a kind of despair, I asked the Lord to fill me with the Holy Spirit; and the moment I did this . . . I began to see myself and what a selfish ambition I had."

But he did not yet receive the blessing sought. He landed in India and went with a fellow missionary to an open-air service. "The missionary spoke," said John Hyde, "and I was told that he was speaking about Jesus Christ as the real Savior from sin. When he had finished his address, a respectable-looking man, speaking good English, asked the missionary whether he himself had been thus saved? The question went home to my heart; for if it had been asked me, I would have had to confess that Christ had not fully saved me, because I knew there was a sin in my life that had not been taken away. I realized what a dishonor it would be on the name of Christ to have to confess that I was preaching a Christ that had not delivered me from sin, though I was proclaiming to others that He was a perfect Savior. I went back to my room and shut myself in and told the Lord that it must be one of two things: either He must give me victory over all my sins, and especially over the sin that so easily beset me, or I must return to America and seek there for some other work. I said I could not stand up to preach the Gospel until I could testify of its power in my life.

I . . . realized how reasonable this was, and the Lord assured me that He was able and willing to deliver me from all sin. He did deliver me, and I have not had a doubt of this since."

It was then and then only that John Hyde became Praying Hyde. And it is only by such a full surrender and such a definite claiming to be delivered from the power of sin in our lives that you and I can be people of prevailing prayer.

The point we wish to emphasize, however, is the one already mentioned. A comparatively unknown man prays for John Hyde, who was then unknown to the world, and by his prayer brings down such a blessing upon him that everyone knows of him now as "Praying Hyde." Did you say in your heart, dear reader, a little while ago, that you could not hope to be Praying Hyde? Of course we cannot all give so much time to prayer. For physical or other reasons we may be hindered from long-continued praying. But we may all have his spirit of prayer. And may we not all do for others what the unnamed friend did for John Hyde?

Can we not pray the blessing down upon others, upon your vicar or pastor? Upon your friend? Upon your family? What a ministry is ours, if we will but enter it! But to do so, we must make the full surrender that John Hyde made. Have we not done it?

Failure in prayer is due to fault in the heart. Only the "pure in heart" can see God. And only those who "call on the Lord out of a pure heart" (2 Tim. 2:22) can confidently claim answers to their prayers.

What a revival would break out, what a mighty blessing would come down if only everyone who reads these words would claim the fullness of the Holy Spirit now!

Do you not see why it is that God wants us to pray? Do you now see why everything worth having depends upon prayer? There are several reasons, but one stands out very clearly and vividly before us after reading this chapter. It is just this: if we ask and God does not give, then the fault is with us.

Every unanswered prayer is a clarion call to search the heart to see what is wrong there, for the promise is unmistakable in its clearness: "If ye shall ask anything in My name, that will I do" (John 14:14).

Truly he who prays puts not God but his own spiritual life
to the test!

> Let me come closer to Thee, Jesus,
>   Oh, closer every day;
> Let me lean hard on Thee, Jesus,
>   Yes, harder all the way.

Chapter 4

Asking for Signs

"Does God indeed answer prayer?" is a question often on the lips of people and oftener still in their inmost hearts. "Is prayer of any real use?" Somehow or other we cannot help praying. But then even pagan savages cry out to someone or something to aid them in times of danger and disaster and distress.

And those of us who really do believe in prayer are soon faced with another question: "Is it right to put God to the test?" Moreover, a further thought flashes into our minds: "Dare we put God to the test?" For there is little doubt that failure in the prayer life is often—always?—due to failure in the spiritual life. So many people harbor much unbelief in the heart regarding the value and effectiveness of prayer. Without faith, prayer is vain.

Asking for signs? Putting God to the test? Would to God we could persuade Christian men and women to do so. Why, what a test this would be of our own faith in God and of our own holiness of life. Prayer is the touchstone of true godliness. God asks for our prayers, values our prayers, needs our prayers. And if those prayers fail, we have only ourselves to blame. We do not mean by this that effective prayer always gets just what it asks for. Now, the Bible teaches us that we are allowed to put God to the test. The example of Gideon in Old Testament days is sufficient to show us that God honors our faith even when that faith is faltering. He allows us to "prove Him" even after a definite promise from Himself. This is a very great comfort to us.

Gideon said unto God, "If Thou wilt save Israel by mine hand, as Thou hast said, behold, I will put a fleece of wool on the floor; and if the dew be on the fleece only . . . then shall I know that Thou wilt save Israel by mine hand, as Thou has said" (Judges 6:36, 37).Yet, although there was a "bowl full of water" in the fleece the next morning, this did not satisfy Gideon! He dares to put God to the test the second time and to ask that the fleece should be dry instead of wet the following night. "And God did so that night" (Judges 6:40).

It is all very wonderful, the Almighty God just doing what a hesitating man asks Him to do! We catch our breath and stand amazed, scarcely knowing which startles us the more: the daring of the man or the condescension of God! Of course, there is more in the story than meets the eye. No doubt Gideon thought that the "fleece" represented himself, Gideon.

If God would indeed fill him with His Spirit, why, salvation was assured. But as he wrung the fleece out, he began to compare himself with the saturated wool. "How unlike this fleece am I! God promises deliverance, but I do not feel full of the Spirit of God. No inflow of the mighty power of God seems to have come into me. Am I indeed fit for this great feat?" No! But then, it is "Not I, but God." "O God, let the fleece be dry—canst Thou still work? Even if I do not feel any superhuman power, any fullness of spiritual blessing within me; even if I feel as dry as this fleece, canst Thou still deliver Israel by my arm?" (Little wonder that he prefaced his prayer with the words "Let not Thine anger be hot against me"!) "And God did so that night: for it was dry upon the fleece only, and there was dew on all the ground" (v. 40).

Yes, there is more in the story than can be seen at a glance. And is it not so in our own case? The Devil so often assures us that our prayers cannot claim an answer because of the "dryness" of our souls. Answers to prayer, however, do not depend upon our feelings but upon the trustworthiness of the Promiser.

Now, we are not urging that Gideon's way of procedure is for us, or for anyone, the normal course of action. It seems to reveal much hesitation to believe God's Word. In fact, it looks gravely like doubting God. And surely it grieves God when we show a faith in Him that is but partial.

The higher and better and safer way is to "ask, nothing doubting." But it is very comforting and assuring to us to know that God allowed Gideon to put Him to the test. Nor is this the only such case mentioned in Scripture. The most surprising instance of "proving God" happened on the Sea of Galilee. St. Peter put our Lord Himself to the test. "If it be Thou . . ." yet our Savior had already said, "It is I." "If it be Thou, bid me come unto Thee on the water." And our Lord said, "Come," and Peter "walked on the water" (Matt. 14:28–29). But this "testing-faith" of Peter's soon failed him. "Little faith" (v. 31) so often and so quickly becomes "doubt." Remember that Christ did not reprove him for coming. Our Lord did not say, "Wherefore didst thou come?" but "Wherefore didst thou doubt?"

To put God to the test is, after all, not the best method. He has given us so many promises contingent on believing prayer and has so often proved His power and His willingness to answer prayer, that we ought, as a rule, to hesitate very much before we ask Him for signs as well as for wonders!

But, someone may be thinking, does not the Lord God Almighty Himself bid us to put Him to the test? Did He not say, "Bring ye the whole tithe into the storehouse . . . and prove Me now herewith, saith the Lord of Hosts, if I will not open unto you the windows of heaven, and pour you out a blessing, that there shall not be room enough to receive it" (Mal. 3:10)?

Yes, that is true. God does say, "Prove Me; test Me." But it is really we ourselves who are thus tested. If the windows of heaven are not opened when we pray, and this blessing of fullness-to-overflowing is not bestowed upon us, it can only be because we are not whole-tithers. When we are indeed wholly yielded to God, when we have brought the whole tithe into the storehouse for God, we shall find such a blessing that we shall not need to put God to any test! This is a thing we shall have to speak about when we come to the question of unanswered prayer.

Meanwhile we want every Christian to ask, "Have I ever fairly tested prayer?" How long is it since you last offered up a definite prayer? People pray for "a blessing" upon an address or a meeting or a mission, and some blessing is certain to come, for others are also pleading with God about the matter. You ask for relief from pain or healing of sickness, but godless people, for whom no one appears to be praying, often recover and sometimes in a seemingly miraculous way. And we may feel that we might have got better even if no prayer had been offered on our behalf. It seems to me that so many people cannot put their finger upon any really definite and conclusive answer to prayer in their own experience. Most Christians do not give God a chance to show His delight in granting His children's petitions, for their requests are so vague and indefinite. If this is so, it is not surprising that prayer is so often a mere form, an almost mechanical repetition, day by day, of certain phrases, a few minutes' "exercise" morning and evening.

Then there is another point. Have you, when in prayer, ever had the witness borne in upon you that your request was granted? Those who know something of the private life of people of prayer are often amazed at the complete assurance that comes over them at times that their prayers are answered, long before the boon they seek is actually in their possession. One prayer warrior would say, "A peace came over my soul. I was confident my request was granted me." He then just thanked God for what he was quite sure God had done for him. And his assurance would prove to be absolutely well founded.

Our Lord Himself always had this assurance, and we should ever bear in mind that, although He was God, He lived His earthly life as a perfect Man, depending upon the Holy Spirit of God.

When He stood before the opened tomb of Lazarus before He had actually called upon the dead to come forth, He had said, "Father, I thank Thee that Thou has heard Me. And I know that Thou hearest Me always" (John 11:41–42). Why then did He utter His thanks? "Because of the people which stand by I said it, that they may believe that Thou has sent Me." If Christ is dwelling in our hearts by faith, if the Holy Spirit is breathing into us our petitions, and if we are "praying in the Holy Ghost," ought we not to know that the Father "hears" us (Jude 20)? And will not those who stand by begin to recognize that we, too, are God-sent?

Men of prayer and women of prayer will agonize before God for something that they know is according to His will, because of some definite promise on the page of Scripture. They may pray for hours, or even for days, when suddenly the Holy Spirit reveals to them in no uncertain way that God has granted their request. They are then confident that they need no longer send up any more petitions to God about the matter. It is as if God said in clear tones: "Thy prayer is heard and I have granted thee the desire of thy heart." This is not the experience of only one man, but most men to whom prayer is the basis of their life will bear witness to the same fact. Nor is it a solitary experience in their lives. It occurs again and again.

Then prayer must give place to action. God taught Moses this: "Wherefore criest thou unto Me? Speak unto the children of Israel that they go forward" (Exod. 14:15).

We are not surprised to find that Dr. Goforth, a much-used missionary in China, often had this assurance given him that his petitions were granted. "I knew that God had answered. I received definite assurance that He would open the way." For why should anyone be surprised at this? The Lord Jesus said, "Ye are My friends, if ye do the things I command you. No longer do I call you servants; for the servant knoweth not what his lord doeth: but I have called you friends" (John 15:14–15). Do you think it surprising, then, if the Lord lets us, His "friends," know something of His plans and purposes?

The question at once arises, "Does God mean this to be the experience of only a few chosen saints, or does He wish all believers to exercise a like faith and to have a like assurance that their prayers are answered?"

We know that God is no respecter of persons, and therefore we know that any true believer in Him may share His mind and will. We are His friends if we do the things He commands us. One of those things is "prayer." Our Savior begged His disciples to "have faith in God" (the literal translation is "Have the faith of God"). Then, He declares, you can say to a mountain, "Be thou taken up and cast into the sea," and if you believe and doubt not, it shall come to pass. Then He gives this promise: "All things whatsoever ye pray and ask for, believe that ye have received them [that is, in heaven], and ye shall have them [on earth]" (Mark 11:24). Now, this is exactly the experience we have been talking about. This is just what real people of prayer do. Such things naturally pass the comprehension of unbelievers. Such things are perplexing to the half-believers. Our Lord, however, desires that men should know that we are His disciples, sent as He was sent (John 17:18; 20:21). They will know this if we love one another (John 13:35). But another proof is provided, and it is this: if we know and they see that "God heareth us always" (John 11:42).

Some of us at once recall to mind George Müller's wonderful prayer life. On one occasion, when crossing from Quebec to Liverpool, he had prayed very definitely that a chair he had ordered should arrive from New York in time to catch the steamer, and he was quite confident that God had granted his petition. About half an hour before the tender was timed to take the passengers to the ship, the agents informed him that no chair had arrived and that it could not possibly come in time for the steamer. Now, Mrs. Müller suffered much from sea-sickness, and it was absolutely essential that she should have the chair. Yet nothing would induce Mr. Müller to buy another one from a shop near by. "We have made a special prayer that our Heavenly Father would be pleased to provide it for us, and we will trust Him to do so," was his reply, and he went on board absolutely sure that his trust was not misplaced and would not miscarry. Just before the tender left, a van drove up, and on the top of it was Mr. Müller's chair. It was hurried on board and placed into the hands of the very man who had urged

George Müller to buy another one! When he handed it to Mr. Müller, the latter expressed no surprise but quietly removed his hat and thanked his Heavenly Father. To this man of God such an answer to prayer was not wonderful but natural. And do you not think that God allowed the chair to be held back till the very last minute as a lesson to Mrs. Müller's friends—and to us? We should never have heard of that incident but for that delay.

God does all He can to induce us to pray and to trust, and yet how slow we are to do so! Oh, what we miss through lack of faith and want of prayer! No one can have very real and deep communion with God who does not know how to pray so as to get answers to prayer.

If one has any doubt as to God's willingness to be put to the test, let him read a little book called *Nor Scrip* (Marshall, Morgan, and Scott, Ltd.). Miss Amy Wilson Carmichael tells us in its pages how again and again she "proved God." One gets the impression from the book that it was no accident that led her to do so. Surely God's hand was in it? For instance, to rescue a Hindu child from a life of "religious" shame, it was necessary to spend a hundred rupees. Was she justified in doing so? She could help many girls for such a sum; ought she to spend it on one? Miss Wilson Carmichael felt led to pray that God would send her the round sum of a hundred rupees—no more, no less—if it was His will that the money should be spent in this way. The money came—the exact amount—and the sender of it explained that she had sat down to write a check for a broken sum but had been impelled to make it just a hundred rupees.

That happened over fifteen years ago, and since that time this same missionary has put God to the test over and over again, and He has never failed her. This is what she says: "Never once in fifteen years has a bill been left unpaid; never once has a man or woman been told when we were in need of help; but never once have we lacked any good thing. Once, as if to show what could be done if it were required, £25 came by telegram! Sometimes a man would emerge from the clamoring crowd at a railway station, slip some indispensable gift of money into the hand, and be lost in the crowd again before the giver could be indentified."

Is it wonderful? Wonderful! Why, what does St. John say, speaking by the Spirit of God? "And this is the boldness which we have towards Him, that if we ask anything, according to His will, he heareth us; and if we know that He heareth us, whatsover we ask, we know that we have the petitions which we have asked of Him" (1 John 5:14—15). Have you and I such "boldness"? If not, why not?

To call it wonderful is to show our want of faith. It is natural to God to answer prayer; it is normal, not extraordinary. The fact is—so many of us do not believe God. We may just as well be quite candid about it. If we love God we ought to pray, because He wants us to pray and commands us to pray. If we believe God we shall pray because we cannot help doing so; we cannot get on without it. Fellow Christian, you believe in God, and you believe on Him (John 3:16), but have you advanced far enough in the Christian life to believe Him, that is, to believe what He says and all He says? Does it not sound blasphemous to ask such a thing of a Christian person? Yet how few believers really believe God? God forgive us! Has it ever struck you that we trust the word of our fellow human being more easily than we trust God's word? And yet, when a man does "believe God," what miracles of grace God works in and through him! No man ever lived who has been revered and respected by so many peoples and tongues as that man of whom we are told three times over in the New Testament that "he believed God" (Rom. 4:3; Gal. 3:6; James 2:23). Yes, "Abraham believed God, and it was reckoned unto him for righteousness." And today Christians all over the world vie with each other in honoring his name. We implore every believer on Christ Jesus never to rest till he can say, "I believe God and will act on that belief" (Acts 27:25).

But before we leave the question of testing God, we should like to point out that sometimes God leads us on "to prove Him." Sometimes God has put it into the heart of Miss Wilson Carmichael to ask for things she saw no need for. Yet she felt impelled by the Holy Spirit to ask. Not only were they granted her, but they also proved an inestimable boon. Yes, God knows what things we have need of, whether we want them or not, before we ask (Matt. 6:8). Has not God said, "I will in no wise fail thee"?

Often the temptation would come to Miss Wilson Carmichael to let others know of some special need. But always the inner assurance would come, as in the very voice of God, "I know, and that is enough." And, of course, God was glorified. During the trying days of the war, even the heathen used to say, "Their God feeds them." "Is it now known all the country round," said a worldly heathen, "that your God hears prayer?"

Oh, what glory to God was brought about by their simple faith! Why do we not believe God? Why do we not take God at His word? Do believers or unbelievers ever say of us, "We know your prayers are answered"? Ye missionaries the wide world over, listen! (Oh, that these words might reach every ear and stir every heart!) It is the yearning desire of God, of our loving Savior Jesus Christ, that every one of us should have the same strong faith as that devoted lady missionary we are speaking about.

Our loving Father does not wish any child of His to have one moment's anxiety or one unsatisfied need. No matter how great our need may be, no matter how numerous our requirements, if we only "prove Him" in the manner He bids us, we shall never have room enough to receive all the blessing He will give (Mal. 3:10).

> Oh, what peace we often forfeit!
> Oh, what needless pain we bear!
> All because we do not carry
> Everything to God in prayer;

. . . or all because, when we do "carry it," we do not believe God's word. Why is it we find it so hard to trust Him? Has He ever failed us? Has He not said over and over again that He will grant all petitions offered out of a pure heart, "in His name"? "Ask of Me," "Pray ye," "Prove Me," "Try Me." The Bible is full of answers to prayer, wonderful answers, miraculous answers. And yet somehow our faith fails us, and we dishonor God by distrusting Him!

If our faith were but more simple
We should take Him at His word,
And our lives would be all sunshine
In the bounties of our Lord.

But our eye must be "single" if our faith is to be simple
and our "whole body full of light" (Matt. 6:22). Christ must
be the sole Master. We cannot expect to be free from anxiety
if we are trying to serve God and Mammon (Matt. 6:24–25).
Again we are led back to the Victorious Life! When we indeed
present our bodies "a living sacrifice, holy, acceptable to
God" (Rom. 12:1); when we present our members "as
servants to righteousness and sanctification" (Rom. 6:19);
then He presents Himself to us and fills us with all the
fullness of God (Eph. 3:19).

Let us ever bear in mind that real faith not only believes
that God can but that He does answer prayer. We may be
slothful in prayer, but "the Lord is not slack concerning His
promise" (2 Peter 3:9). Is not that a striking expression?

Perhaps the most extraordinary testing of God that this
Dohnavur missionary tells us of is the following: The
question arose of purchasing a rest-house in the hills
nearby. Was it the right thing to do? Only God could decide.
Much prayer was made. Eventually the petition was offered
up that if it was God's will that the house should be
purchased, the exact sum of £100 should be received. That
amount came at once. Yet they still hesitated. Two months
later they asked God to give them again the same sign of His
approval of the purchase. That same day another check for
£100 came. Even now they scarcely liked to proceed in the
matter. In a few days' time, however, another round sum of
£100 was received, earmarked for the purchase of such a
house. Does it not flood our hearts with joy to remember
that our gracious Savior is so kind? It is St. Luke the
physician who tells us that God is kind (Luke 6:35). Love is
always "kind" (1 Cor. 13:4), and God is Love. Think over it
when you pray. Our Lord is "kind." It will help us in our
intercessions. He bears so patiently with us when our faith
would falter. "How precious is Thy lovingkindness, O God"

(Ps. 36:7); "Thy lovingkindness is better than life" (Ps. 63:3).

The danger is that we read of such simple faith in prayer and say, "How wonderful!" and forget that God desires every one of us to have such faith and such prayer. God has no favorites! He wants me to pray; He wants you to pray. He allows such things to happen as we have described above and suffers them to come to our knowledge, not to surprise us but to stimulate us. One sometimes wishes that Christian people would forget all the man-made rules with which we have hedged about prayer! Let us be simple. Let us be natural. Take God at His word. Let us remember that "the kindness of God our Savior, and His love toward man," has appeared (Titus 3:4). God sometimes leads men into the prayer life. Sometimes, however, God has to drive us into such a life.

As some of us look back over our comparatively prayerless life, what a thrill of wonder and of joy comes over us as we think of the kindness and "patience of Christ" (2 Thess. 3:5). Where should we have been without that? We fail Him, but blessed be His name, He has never failed us, and He never will do so. We doubt Him; we mistrust His love and His providence and His guidance; we "faint because of the way"; we murmur because of the way; yet all the time He is there blessing us and waiting to pour out upon us a blessing so great that there shall not be room to receive it.

The promise of Christ still holds good: "Whatsoever ye shall ask in My name, that will I do, that the Father may be glorified in the Son" (John 14:13).

> Prayer changes things—and yet how blind
> And slow we are to taste and see
> The blessedness that comes to those
>   Who trust in Thee.

But henceforth we will just believe God.

Chapter 5

What Is Prayer?

Mr. Moody was once addressing a crowded meeting of children in Edinburgh. To get their attention he began with a question: "What is prayer?"—looking for no reply and expecting to give the answer himself.

To his amazement scores of little hands shot up all over the hall. He asked one lad to reply, and the answer came at once, clear and correct: "Prayer is an offering up of our desires unto God for things agreeable to His will, in the name of Christ, with confession of our sins and thankful acknowledgment of His mercies." Mr. Moody's delighted comment was, "Thank God, my boy, that you were born in Scotland." But that was half a century ago. What sort of answer would he get today? How many English children could give a definition of prayer? Think for a moment and decide what answer you yourself would give.

What do we mean by prayer? I believe the vast majority of Christians would say, "Prayer is asking things from God." But surely prayer is much more than merely "getting God to run our errands for us," as someone puts it. It is a higher thing than the beggar knocking at the rich man's door.

The word "prayer" really means "a wish directed toward," that is, toward God. All that true prayer seeks is God Himself, for with Him we get all we need. Prayer is simply "the turning of the soul to God." David describes it as the lifting up of the living soul to the living God. "Unto Thee, O

Lord, do I lift up my soul" (Ps. 25:1). What a beautiful description of prayer that is! When we desire the Lord Jesus to behold our souls, we also desire that the beauty of holiness may be upon us. When we lift up our souls to God in prayer it gives God an opportunity to do what He will in us and with us. It is putting ourselves at God's disposal. God is always on our side, but we are not always on His side. When man prays, it is God's opportunity. The poet says:

> Prayer is the soul's sincere desire,
> Uttered or unexpressed,
> The motion of a hidden fire
> That trembles in the breast.

"Prayer," says an old Jewish mystic, "is the moment when heaven and earth kiss each other."

Prayer, then, is certainly not persuading God to do what we want Him to do. It is not bending the will of a reluctant God to our will. It does not change His purpose, although it may release His power. "We must not conceive of prayer as overcoming God's reluctance," says Archbishop Trench, "but as laying hold of His highest willingness."

For God always purposes our greatest good. Even the prayer offered in ignorance and blindness cannot swerve Him from that, although when we persistently pray for some harmful thing, our willfulness may bring it about, and we suffer accordingly. "He gave them their request," says the psalmist, "but sent leanness into their soul" (Ps. 106:15). They brought this "leanness" upon themselves. They were "cursed with the burden of a granted prayer."

Prayer, in the minds of some people, is only for emergencies! Danger threatens, sickness comes, things are lacking, difficulties arise—then they pray. Like the infidel down a coal mine: when the roof began to fall he began to pray. An old Christian standing by quietly remarked, "Aye, there's nowt like cobs of coal to make a man pray."

Prayer is, however, much more than merely asking God for something, although that is a very valuable part of prayer if only because it reminds us of our utter dependence upon God. It is also communion with God, intercourse with

God, talking with (not only to) God. We get to know people by talking with them. We get to know God in like manner. The highest result of prayer is not deliverance from evil or the securing of some coveted thing, but knowledge of God. "And this is life eternal, that they should know Thee, the only true God" (John 17:3). Yes, prayer discovers more of God, and that is the soul's greatest discovery. Men still cry out, "O, that I knew where I might find Him, that I might come even to His seat" (Job 23:3).

The kneeling Christian always "finds" Him and is found of Him. The heavenly vision of the Lord Jesus blinded the eyes of Saul of Tarsus on his downward course, but he tells us, later on, that when he was praying in the temple at Jerusalem he fell into a trance and saw Jesus. "I . . . saw him" (Acts 22:18). Then it was that Christ gave him his great commission to go to the Gentiles. Vision is always a precursor of vocation and venture. It was so with Isaiah. "I saw the Lord high and lifted up, and his train filled the temple" (Isa. 6:1). The prophet was evidently in the sanctuary praying when this happened. This vision also was a prelude to a call to service, "Go . . . ." Now, we cannot get a vision of God unless we pray. And where there is no vision the soul perishes.

A vision of God! Brother Lawrence once said, "Prayer is nothing else than a sense of God's presence," and that is just the practice of the presence of God.

A friend of Horace Bushnell was present when that man of God prayed. There came over him a wonderful sense of God's nearness. He says: "When Horace Bushnell buried his face in his hands and prayed, I was afraid to stretch out my hand in the darkness, lest I should touch God." Was the psalmist of old conscious of such a thought when he cried, "My soul, wait thou only upon God" (Ps. 62:5)? I believe that much of our failure in prayer is due to the fact that we have not looked into this question, "What is prayer?" It is good to be conscious that we are always in the presence of God. It is better to gaze upon Him in adoration. But it is best of all to commune with Him as a Friend, and that is prayer.

Real prayer at its highest and best reveals a soul athirst

for God—just for God alone. Real prayer comes from the lips of those whose affection is set on things above. What a man of prayer Zinzendorf was. Why? He sought the Giver rather than His gifts. He said: "I have one passion: it is He, He alone." Even the Mohammedan seems to express something of this thought. He says that there are three degrees in prayer. The lowest is that spoken only by the lips. The next is when, by a resolute effort, we succeed in fixing our thoughts on Divine things. The third is when the soul finds it hard to turn away from God. Of course, we know that God bids us "ask" of Him. We all obey Him so far, and we may rest well assured that prayer both pleases God and supplies all our need. But he would be a strange child who only sought his father's presence when he desired some gift from him! And do we not all yearn to rise to a higher level of prayer than mere petition? How is it to be done?

It seems to me that only two steps are necessary, or shall we say two thoughts? There must be, first of all, a realization of God's glory and then of God's grace. We sometimes sing:

> Grace and glory flow from Thee;
> Shower, O shower them, Lord, on me.

Nor is such a desire fanciful, although some may ask what God's glory has to do with prayer.

But ought we not to remind ourselves Who He is to Whom we pray? There is logic in the couplet:

> Thou art coming to a King;
> Large petitions with thee bring.

Do you think that any one of us spends enough time pondering and marveling over God's exceeding great glory? And do you suppose that any one of us has grasped the full meaning of the word "grace"? Are not our prayers so often ineffective and powerless because we rush unthinkingly and unpreparedly into God's presence, without realizing the majesty and glory of the God Whom we are approaching and without reflecting upon the exceeding great riches of His glory in Christ Jesus, which we hope to draw upon? We must "think magnificently of God."

May we then suggest that before we lay our petitions before God we first dwell in meditation upon His glory and then upon His grace, for He offers us both. We must lift up the soul to God. Let us place ourselves, as it were, in the presence of God and direct our prayer to the "King of kings, and Lord of lords, Who only hath immortality, dwelling in light unapproachable . . . to Whom be honor and power eternal" (1 Tim. 6:16). Let us then give Him adoration and praise because of His exceeding great glory. Consecration is not enough. There must be adoration.

"Holy, holy, holy, is the Lord of Hosts," cry the seraphim; "the whole earth is full of his glory" (Isa. 6:3). "Glory to God in the highest," cries the "whole multitude of the heavenly host" (Luke 2:14). Yet some of us try to commune with God without stopping to "put off our shoes from off our feet" (Exod. 3:5).

> Lips cry "God be merciful"
> That ne'er cry "God be praised."
>
> O come let us adore Him!

And we may approach His glory with boldness. Did not our Lord pray that His disciples might behold His glory (John 17:24)? Why? And why is "the whole earth full of His glory"? The telescope reveals His infinite glory. The microscope reveals His uttermost glory. Even the unaided eye sees surpassing glory in landscape, sunshine, sea, and sky. What does it all mean? These things are but a partial revelation of God's glory. It was not a desire for self-display that led our Lord to pray, "Father, glorify Thy Son" . . . "O Father, glorify Thou Me" (John 17:1, 5). Our dear Lord wants us to realize His infinite trustworthiness and unlimited power, so that we can approach Him in simple faith and trust.

In heralding the coming of Christ the prophet declared that "the glory of the Lord shall be revealed, and all flesh shall see it together" (Isa. 40:5). Now we must get a glimpse of that glory before we can pray aright. So our Lord said, "When ye pray, say Our Father, Who art in heaven [the realm of glory], hallowed be Thy name." There is nothing like a glimpse of glory to banish fear and doubt. Before we offer up our petitions, may it not help us to offer up our adoration in the words of praise used by some of the saints of old? Some devout souls may not need such help. We are told that Francis of Assisi would frequently spend an hour or two in prayer on the top of Mount Averno, where the only word that escaped his lips would be "God" repeated at intervals. He began with adoration and often stopped there!

But most of us need some help to realize the glory of the invisible God before we can adequately praise and adore Him. Old William Law said, "When you begin to pray, use such expressions of the attributes of God as will make you sensible of His greatness and power."

This point is of such tremendous importance that we venture to remind our readers of helpful words. Some of us begin every day with a glance heavenward while saying, "Glory be to the Father, and to the Son, and to the Holy Ghost." The prayer, "O Lord God most holy, O Lord most mighty, O holy and merciful Savior!" is often enough to bring a solemn awe and a spirit of holy adoration upon the soul. The Gloria in Excelsis of the Communion Service is most uplifting: "Glory be to God on high and on earth peace. . . . We praise Thee; we bless Thee; we worship Thee; we glorify Thee; we give thanks to Thee for Thy great glory, O Lord God, heavenly King, God the Father Almighty." Which of us can from the heart utter praise like that and remain unmoved, unconscious of the very presence and wondrous majesty of the Lord God Almighty? A verse of a hymn may serve the same purpose.

> My God, how wonderful Thou art!
> Thy majesty how bright.
> How beautiful Thy mercy-seat
> In depths of burning light!
> How wonderful, how beautiful
> The sight of Thee must be;
> Thine endless wisdom, boundless power
> And awful purity.

This carries us into the very heavenlies, as also do the words:

> Holy, holy, holy, Lord God Almighty,
> All Thy works shall praise Thy name
> In earth, and sky, and sea.

We need to cry out, and to cry often, "My soul doth magnify the Lord, and my spirit hath rejoiced in God my Savior" (Luke 1:46–47). Can we catch the spirit of the psalmist and sing, "Bless the Lord, O my soul, and all that is within me, bless His holy name" (Ps. 103:1)? "Bless the Lord, O my soul. O Lord my God, Thou art very great; Thou art clothed with honor and majesty" (Ps. 104:1). When shall we learn that "in His temple everything saith Glory!" (Ps. 29:9 RV). Let us too cry, Glory!

Such worship of God, such adoration and praise and thanksgiving, not only put us into the spirit of prayer, but in some mysterious way they help God to work on our behalf. Do you remember those wonderful words, "Whoso offereth the sacrifice of thanksgiving, glorifyeth Me and prepareth a way that I may show him the salvation of God" (Ps. 50:23 RV marg.)? Praise and thanksgiving not only open the gates of heaven for me to approach God but also "prepare a way" for God to bless me. St. Paul cries, "Rejoice evermore! before he says, "Pray without ceasing." So then our praise, as well as our prayers, is to be without ceasing.

At the raising of Lazarus our Lord's prayer had as its first utterance a note of thanksgiving. "Father, I thank Thee that Thou heardest Me" (John 11:41). He said it for those around to hear. Yes, and for us to hear.

You may perhaps be wondering why it is that we should especially give thanks to God for His great glory when we kneel in prayer, and why we should spend any time in thinking of and gazing upon that glory. But is He not the King of Glory? All He is and all He does is glory. His holiness is glorious (Exod. 15:11). His name is glorious (Deut. 28:58). His work is glorious (Ps. 111:3). His power is glorious (Col. 1:11). His voice is glorious (Isa. 30:30).

All things bright and beautiful
All creatures great and small.
All things wise and wonderful,
The Lord God made them all.

And He made them for His glory.

"For of him and through him and unto him are all things;
to whom be glory for ever" (Rom. 11:36). And this is the God
who bids us come to Him in prayer. This God is our God,
and He has "gifts for prayer." This God is our God, and He
has "gifts for men" (Ps. 68:18). God says that everyone that
is called by His name has been created for His glory (Isa.
43:7). His Church is to be a "glorious" Church, holy and
without blemish (Eph. 5:27). Have you ever fully realized
that the Lord Jesus desires to share with us the glory we see
in Him? This is His great gift to you and me, His redeemed
ones. Believe me, the more we have of God's glory, the less
shall we seek His gifts. Not only in that day "when He shall
come to be glorified in His saints" (2 Thess. 1:10) is there
glory for us, but here and now, today. He wishes us to be
partakers of His glory. Did not our Lord Himself say so?
"The glory which Thou has given Me, I have given unto
them," He declares (John 17:22). What is God's command?
"Arise, shine, for thy light is come, and the glory of the Lord
is risen upon thee." Nay, more than this: "His glory shall be
seen upon thee," says the inspired prophet (Isa. 60:1–2).

God would have people say of us as St. Peter said of the
disciples of old: "The Spirit of glory and the Spirit of God
resteth upon you" (1 Peter 4:14). Would not that be an
answer to most of our prayers? Could we ask for anything
better? How can we get this glory? How are we to reflect it?
Only as the result of prayer. It is when we pray that the Holy
Spirit takes of the things of Christ and reveals them unto us
(John 16:15).

It was when Moses prayed, "Show me, I pray thee, thy
glory," that he not only saw something of it but shared
something of that glory, and his own face shone with the
light of it (Exod. 33:18; 34:29). And when we, too, gaze
upon the "glory of God in the face of Jesus Christ" (2 Cor.

4:6), we shall see not only a glimpse of that glory, but we shall gain something of it ourselves.

Now, that is prayer and the highest result of prayer. Nor is there any other way of securing that glory, that God may be glorified in us (Isa. 60:21).

Let us often meditate upon Christ's glory, gaze upon it and so reflect it and receive it. This is what happened to our Lord's first disciples. They said in awed tones, "We beheld his glory!" Yes, but what followed? A few plain, unlettered, obscure fishermen accompanied Christ a little while, seeing His glory, and lo! they themselves caught something of that glory. And then others marveled and "took knowledge of them that they had been with Jesus" (Acts 4:13). And when we can declare, with St. John, "Yea and our fellowship is with the Father and with His Son Jesus Christ" (1 John 1:3), people will say the same of us: "They have been with Jesus!"

As we lift up our soul in prayer to the living God, we gain the beauty of holiness as surely as a flower becomes beautiful by living in the sunlight. Was not our Lord Himself transfigured when He prayed? And the "very fashion" of our countenance will change, and we shall have our Mount of Transfiguration when prayer has its rightful place in our lives. And men will see in our faces "the outward and visible sign of an inward and spiritual grace." Our value to God and to man is in exact proportion to the extent in which we reveal the glory of God to others.

We have dwelt so much upon the glory of Him to Whom we pray, that we must now speak of His grace.

What is prayer? It is a sign of spiritual life. I should as soon expect life in a dead man as spiritual life in a prayerless soul! Our spirituality and our fruitfulness are always in proportion to the reality of our prayers. If, then, we have at all wandered away from home in the matter of prayer, let us today resolve, "I will arise and go unto my Father, and say unto Him, Father . . ."

At this point I laid down my pen, and on the page of the first paper I picked up were these words: "The secret of failure is that we see men rather than God. Romanism trembled when Martin Luther saw God. The 'great awakening' sprang into being when Jonathan Edwards saw God. The world became the parish of one man when John Wesley saw God. Multitudes were saved when Whitfield saw God. Thousands of orphans were fed when George Müller saw God. And He is 'the same yesterday, today, and forever.' "

Is it not time that we got a new vision of God—in all His glory? Who can say what will happen when the Church sees God? But let us not wait for others. Let us, each one for himself, with unveiled face and unsullied heart, get this vision of the glory of the Lord.

"Blessed are the pure in heart, for they shall see God" (Matt. 5:8). No missionary whom it has been my joy to meet ever impressed me quite as much as Dr. Wilbur Chapman. He wrote to a friend: "I have learned some great lessons concerning prayer. At one of our missions in England the audiences were exceedingly small. But I received a note saying that an American missionary . . . was going to pray God's blessing down upon our work. He was known as 'Praying Hyde.' Almost instantly the tide turned. The hall became packed, and at my first invitation fifty men accepted Christ as their Savior. As we were leaving I said, 'Mr. Hyde, I want you to pray for me.' He came to my room, turned the key in the door, and dropped on his knees, and waited five minutes without a single syllable coming from his lips. I could hear my own heart thumping and beating. I felt the hot tears running down my face. I knew I was with God. Then, with upturned face, down which the tears were streaming, he said 'O God!' Then for five minutes at least he was still again; and then, when he knew that he was talking with God . . . there came up from the depth of his heart such petitions for men as I had never heard before. I rose from my knees to know what real prayer was. We believe that prayer is mighty, and we believe it as we never did before."

Dr. Chapman used to say, "It was a season of prayer with John Hyde that made me realize what real prayer was. I owe to him more than I owe to any man for showing me what a prayer life is and what a real consecrated life is. Jesus

Christ became a new Ideal to me, and I had a glimpse of His prayer life, and I had a longing which has remained to this day to be a real praying man." And God the Holy Spirit can so teach us.

> Oh, ye who sigh and languish
>   And mourn your lack of power,
> Hear ye this gentle whisper:
>   "Could ye not watch one hour?"
> For fruitfulness and blessing
>   There is no royal road;
> The power for holy service
>   Is intercourse with God.

Chapter 6

How Shall I Pray?

How shall I pray? Could there be a more important question for a Christian to ask? How shall I approach the King of Glory?

When we read Christ's promises regarding prayer, we are apt to think that He puts far too great a power into our hands, unless, indeed, we hastily conclude that it is impossible for Him to act as He promises. He says, ask "anything," "whatsoever," "what ye will," and it shall be done.

But then He puts in a qualifying phrase. He says that we are to ask in His name. That is the condition, and the only one; although, as we shall remind ourselves later on, it is sometimes couched in different words.

If, therefore, we ask and do not receive, it can only be that we are not fulfilling this condition. If then we are true disciples of His, if we are sincere, we shall take pains (infinite pains, if need be) to discover just what it means to ask in His name, and we shall not rest content until we have fulfilled that condition. Let us read the promise again to be quite sure about it. "Whatsoever ye shall ask in my name, that will I do, that the Father may be glorified in the Son. If ye shall ask anything in my name, I will do it" (John 14:13–14).

This was something quite new, for our Lord said so. "Hitherto ye have asked nothing in my name," but now, "ask and ye shall receive, that your joy may be full" (John 16:24).

Five times over our Lord repeats this simple condition, "In my name" (John 14:13–14; 15:16; 16:23, 24, 26). Evidently something very important is here implied. It is more than a condition. It is also a promise, an encouragement, for our Lord's biddings are always His enablings. What, then, does it mean to ask in His name? We must know this at all costs, for it is the secret of all power in prayer. And it is possible to make a wrong use of those words. Our Lord said, "Many shall come in my name, saying, 'I am Christ,' and shall deceive many" (Matt. 24:5). He might well have said, "And many shall think they are praying to the Father in my name, while deceiving themselves."

Does it mean just adding the words, "and all this we ask in the name of Jesus Christ," at the end of our prayers?

Many people apparently think that it does. But have you never heard, or offered, prayers full of self-will and selfishness that ended up in that way, "for Christ's sake, amen"?

God could not answer the prayers St. James refers to in his epistle just because those who offered them added, "we ask these things in the name of our Lord Jesus Christ." Those Christians were asking "amiss" (James 4:3). A wrong prayer cannot be made right by the addition of some mystic phrase!

And a right prayer does not fail if some such words are omitted. No! It is more than a question of words. Our Lord is thinking about faith and facts more than about some formula. The chief object of prayer is to glorify the Lord Jesus. We are to ask in Christ's name "that the Father may be glorified in the Son" (John 14:13). Listen! We are not to seek wealth or health, prosperity or success, ease or comfort, spirituality or fruitfulness in service simply for our own enjoyment or advancement or popularity, but only for Christ's sake, for His glory.

Let us take three steps to a right understanding of those important words, "in my name."

I. There is a sense in which some things are done only "for

Christ's sake," because of His atoning death. Those who do not believe in the atoning death of Christ cannot pray "in His name." They may use the words, but without effect. For we are "justified by His blood" (Rom. 5:9), and "we have redemption through His blood, even the forgiveness of sins" (Eph. 1:7; Col. 1:14). In these days when Unitarianism under its guileful name of Modernism has invaded all sects, it is most important to remember the place and work of the shed blood of Christ, or "prayer" (so-called) becomes a delusion and a snare.

Let us illustrate this point by an experience that happened quite early in Mr. Moody's ministry. The wife of an infidel judge, a man of great intellectual gifts, begged Mr. Moody to speak to her husband. Moody, however, hesitated to argue with such a man and told him so quite frankly. "But," he added, "if ever you are converted will you promise to let me know?" The judge laughed cynically and replied, "Oh, yes, I'll let you know quick enough if I am ever converted!" Moody went his way, relying upon prayer. That judge was converted within a year. He kept his promise and told Moody just how it came about. "I began to grow very uneasy and miserable one night when my wife was at a prayer meeting. I went to bed before she came home. I could not sleep all that night. Getting up early the next morning, I told my wife I should not need any breakfast and went to to my office. Telling the clerks they could take a holiday, I shut myself up in my private room. But I became more and more wretched. Finally, I fell on my knees and asked God to forgive me my sins, but I would not say 'for Jesus' sake,' for I was Unitarian, and I did not believe in the atonement. In an agony of mind I kept praying, 'O God, forgive me my sins,' but no answer came. At last, in desperation, I cried, 'O God, for Christ's sake forgive my sins.' Then I found peace at once."

That judge had no access to the presence of God until he sought it in the name of Jesus Christ. When he came in Christ's name he was at once heard and forgiven. Yes, to pray "in the name" of the Lord Jesus is to ask for things that the blood of Christ has secured—"purchased"—for us.

We have "boldness to enter into the holiest by the blood of Jesus" (Heb. 10:19). There is entrance by no other way.

But this is not all that those words "In My Name" mean.

II. The most familiar illustration of coming "in the name" of Christ is that of drawing money from a bank by means of a check. I can draw from my bank account only up to the amount of my deposit there. In my own name, I can go no farther. In the Bank of England I have no money whatsoever and can therefore draw nothing from there. But suppose a very wealthy man who has a big account there gives me a blank check bearing his signature and bids me fill it in to any amount I choose. He is my friend. What shall I do? Shall I just satisfy my present need, or shall I draw as much as I dare? I shall certainly do nothing to offend my friend or to lower myself in his esteem.

Well, we are told by some that heaven is our bank. God is the Great Banker, for "every good gift and every perfect gift is from above, and cometh down from the Father" (James 1:17). We need a "check" wherewith to "draw" upon this boundless store. The Lord Jesus gives us a blank check in prayer. "Fill it in," says He, "to any amount; ask 'anything,' 'what ye will,' and you shall have it. Present your check in My name, and your request will be honored." Let me put this in the words of a well-known evangelist of today. "That is what happens when I go to the bank of heaven—when I go to God in prayer. I have nothing deposited there; I have no credit there; and if I go in my own name I will get absolutely nothing. But Jesus Christ has unlimited credit in heaven, and He has granted me the privilege of going with His name on my checks. And when I thus go my prayers will be honored to any extent. To pray, then, in the name of Christ is to pray, not on the ground of my credit, but His."

This is all very delightful and, in a sense, very true.

If the check were drawn on a Government account or upon some wealthy corporation, one might be tempted to get all one could. But remember we are coming to a loving Father to Whom we owe all, and Whom we love with all our heart, and to Whom we may come repeatedly. In cashing our checks at the bank of heaven we desire chiefly His honor and His glory. We wish to do only that which is pleasing in His sight. To cash certain "checks"—to answer some of our prayers—would only bring dishonor to His name and discredit and discomfort to us. True, His resources are unlimited, but His honor is assailable.

But experience makes argument unnecessary! Dear reader, have we not—all of us—often tried this method only to fail?

How many of us dare say we have never come away from the bank of heaven without getting what we asked for, although we have apparently asked "in Christ's name"? Wherein do we fail? Is it because we do not seek to learn God's will for us? We must not try to exceed His will.

May I give a personal experience of my own that has never been told in public and is probably quite unique? It happened over thirty years ago, and now I see why. It makes such a splendid illustration of what we are now trying to learn about prayer.

A well-to-do friend, who was also an exceedingly busy one, wished to give me one pound toward a certain object. He invited me to his office and hastily wrote out a check for the amount. He folded the check and handed it to me, saying, "I will not cross it. Will you kindly cash it at the bank?" On arriving at the bank I glanced at my name on the check without troubling to verify the amount, endorsed it, and handed it to a clerk. "This is rather a big sum to cash over the counter," he said, eyeing me narrowly. "Yes," I replied laughingly, "one pound!" "No," said the clerk: "this is made out for one thousand pounds!"

And so it was! My friend was, no doubt, accustomed to writing big checks, and he had actually written "one thousand" instead of "one" pound. Now, what was my position legally? The check was truly in his name. The signature was all right. My endorsement was all right. Could I not demand the one thousand pounds, provided there were sufficient funds in the account? The check was written deliberately, if hurriedly, and freely to me. Why should I not take the gift? Why not?

But I was dealing with a friend, a generous friend to whom I owed many deeds of lovingkindness. He had revealed his mind to me. I knew his wishes and desires.

He meant to give me one pound and no more. I knew his intention, his "mind," and at once took back the all-too-generous check, and in due time I received just one pound, according to his will. Had that donor given me a blank check the result would have been exactly the same. He would have expected me to write in one pound, and my honor would have been at stake in my doing so. Need we draw the lesson? God has His will for each one of us, and unless we seek to know that will we are likely to ask for "a thousand," when He knows that "one" will be best for us.

In our prayers we are coming to a Friend, a loving Father. We owe everything to Him. He bids us come to Him whenever we like for all we need. His resources are infinite.

But He bids us to remember that we should ask only for those things that are according to His will, only for what will bring glory to His name. John says, "If we ask anything according to His will, He heareth us" (1 John 5:14). So then our Friend gives us a blank check and leaves us to fill in "anything," but He knows that if we truly love Him we shall never put down—never ask for—things He is not willing to give us because they would be harmful to us.

Perhaps with most of us the fault lies in the other direction. God gives us a blank check and says, "Ask for a pound"—and we ask for a shilling! Would not my friend have been insulted had I treated him thus? Do we ask enough? Do we dare to ask "according to His riches in glory"?

The point we are dwelling upon, however, is this: We cannot be sure that we are praying "in His name" unless we learn His will for us.

III. But even now we have not exhausted the meaning of those words, "In my Name." We all know what it is to ask for a thing "in the name" of another. But we are very careful not to allow anyone to use our name who is not to be trusted, or he might abuse our trust and discredit our name. Gehazi, the trusted servant, dishonestly used Elisha's name. He secured riches but also inherited a curse for his wickedness.

A trusted clerk often uses his employer's name and handles great sums of money as if they were his own. But this he does only so long as he is thought to be worthy of such confidence in him. And he used the money for his master and not for himself. All our money belongs to our Master, Christ Jesus. We can go to God for supplies in His name if we use all we get for His glory.

When I go to cash a check payable to me, the banker is quite satisfied if the signature of his client is genuine and that I am the person authorized to receive the money. He does not ask for references to my character. He has no right whatever to enquire whether I am worthy to receive the money or to be trusted to use it aright. It is not so with the Bank of Heaven. Now, this is a point of greatest importance. Do not hurry over what is now to be said. When I go to heaven's bank in the name of the Lord Jesus, with a check drawn upon the unsearchable riches of Christ, God demands that I shall be a worthy recipient—not "worthy" in the sense that I can merit or deserve anything from a holy God, but worthy in the sense that I am seeking the gift not for my own glory or self-interest, but only for the glory of God.

Otherwise I may pray and not get. "Ye ask and receive not, because ye ask amiss that ye may spend it in your pleasures" (James 4:3 RV).

The great Heavenly Banker will not cash checks for us if our motives are not right. Is not this why so many fail in prayer? Christ's name is the revelation of His character.

To pray "in His name" is to pray in His character, as His representative sent by Him. It is to pray by His Spirit and according to His will; to have His approval in our asking; to seek what He seeks; to ask help to do what He Himself would wish to be done; and to desire to do it not for our own glorification but for His glory alone. To pray "in His name" we must have identity of interests and purpose. Self and its aims and desires must be entirely controlled by God's Holy Spirit, so that our wills are in complete harmony with Christ's will.

We must reach the attitude of St. Augustine when he

cried, "O Lord, grant that I may do Thy will as if it were my will, so that Thou mayest do my will as if it were Thy will."

Child of God, does this seem to make prayer "in His name" quite beyond us? That was not our Lord's intention. He is not mocking us! Speaking of the Holy Spirit, our Lord used these words: "The Comforter . . . Whom the Father will send in my name" (John 14:26). Now, our Savior wants us to be so controlled by the Holy Spirit that we may act in Christ's name. "As many as are led by the Spirit of God, they are the sons of God" (Rom. 8:14). And only sons can say, "Our Father."

Our Lord said of Saul of Tarsus: "He is a chosen vessel unto Me to bear My name before the Gentiles and kings, and the children of Israel" (Acts 9:15). Not to them, but before them. So St. Paul says: "It pleased God to reveal his Son in me." We cannot pray in Christ's name unless we bear that name before people. And this is only possible so long as we "abide in" Him and His words abide in us. So we come to this: Unless the heart is right the prayer must be wrong.

Christ said, "If ye abide in Me, and My words abide in you, ye shall ask what ye will, and it shall be done unto you" (John 15:7).

Those three promises are really identical; they express the same thought in different words. Look at them:

Ask anything in my name, I will do it (John 14:13–14).

Ask what ye will (if ye abide in me and my words abide in you), and it shall be done (John 15:7).

Ask anything, according to his will, we have the petitions (1 John 5:14).

And we could sum them all up in the words of St. John, "Whatsoever we ask, we receive of him, because we keep his commandments and do the things which are pleasing in his sight" (1 John 3:22). When we do what He bids, He does what we ask! Listen to God and God will listen to you. Thus our Lord gives us "power of attorney" over His kingdom, the kingdom of heaven, if only we fulfill the condition of abiding in Him.

Oh, what a wonder is this! How eagerly and earnestly we should seek to know His "mind," His wish, His will! How amazing it is that any one of us should by our own self-seeking miss such unsearchable riches! We know that God's will is the best for us. We know that He longs to bless us and make us a blessing. We know that to follow our own inclination is absolutely certain to harm us and to hurt us and those whom we love. We know that to turn away from His will for us is to court disaster. O child of God, why do we not trust Him fully and wholly? Here we are, then, once again brought face to face with a life of holiness. We see with the utmost clearness that our Savior's call to prayer is simply a clarion call to holiness. "Be ye holy!" for without holiness no man can see God, and prayer cannot be effective.

When we confess that we "never get answers to our prayers," we are condemning not God or His promises or the power of prayer, but ourselves. There is no greater test of spirituality than prayer. The man who tries to pray quickly discovers just where he stands in God's sight.

Unless we are living the Victorious Life we cannot truly pray "in the name" of Christ, and our prayer life must of necessity be feeble, fitful, and often unfruitful.

And "in His name" must be "according to His will." But can we know His will? Assuredly we can. St. Paul not only says, "Let this mind be in you which was in Christ Jesus . . ." (Phil. 2:5); he also boldly declares, "We have the mind of Christ" (1 Cor. 2:16). How, then, can we get to know God's will?

We shall remember that "the secret of the Lord is with them that fear him" (Ps. 25:14).

In the first place, we must not expect God to reveal His will to us unless we desire to know that will and intend to do that will. Knowledge of God's will and the performance of that will go together. We are apt to desire to know God's will so that we may decide whether we will obey or not. Such an attitude is disastrous. "If any man willeth to do His will, he shall know of the teaching" (John 7:17).

God's will is revealed in His Word in Holy Scriptures. What He promises in His Word I may know to be according to His will.

For example, I may confidently ask for wisdom, because His Word says, "If any . . . lack wisdom, let him ask of God . . . and it shall be given him" (James 1:5). We cannot be men of prevailing prayer unless we study God's Word to find out His will for us.

But it is the Holy Spirit of God Who is prayer's great Helper. Read again those wonderful words of St. Paul: "In the same way the Spirit also helps us in our weakness; for we do not know what prayers to offer nor in what way to offer them, but the Spirit Himself pleads for us in yearnings that can find no words, and the Searcher of hearts knows what the Spirit's meaning is, because His intercessions for God's people are in harmony with God's will" (Rom. 8:26–27 WEYMOUTH).

What comforting words! Ignorance and helplessness in prayer are indeed blessed things if they cast us upon the Holy Spirit. Blessed be the name of the Lord Jesus! We are left without excuse. Pray we must: pray we can.

Remember our Heavenly Father is pledged to give the Holy Spirit to them that ask Him (Luke 11:13) and any other "good thing" too (Matt. 7:11).

Child of God, you have often prayed. You have, no doubt, often bewailed your feebleness and slackness in prayer. But have you really prayed in His name?

It is when we have failed and know not "what prayers to offer" or "in what way," that the Holy Spirit is promised as our Helper.

Is it not worth while to be wholly and wholeheartedly yielded to Christ? The half-and-half Christian is of very little use either to God or man. God cannot use him, and man has no use for him but considers him a hypocrite. One sin allowed in the life wrecks at once our usefulness and our joy and robs prayer of its power.

Beloved, we have caught a fresh glimpse of the grace and the glory of our Lord Jesus Christ. He is willing and waiting to share with us both His glory and His grace. He is willing to make us channels of blessing. Shall we not worship God in sincerity and truth, and cry eagerly and earnestly, "Lord, what shall I do?" (Acts. 22:10 RV) and then, in the power of His might, do it?

St. Paul once shot up that prayer to heaven, "What shall I do?" What answer did he get? Listen! He tells us in his counsel to believers everywhere just what it meant to him and should mean to us: "Beloved, put on . . . a heart of compassion, kindness, humility, longsuffering . . . above all things put on love . . . and let the peace of Christ dwell in you richly in all wisdom. . . . And whatsoever ye do, in word or deed, do all in the name of the Lord Jesus, giving thanks to God the Father through Him" (Col. 3:12–17).

It is only when whatsoever we do is done in His name that He will do whatsoever we ask in His name.

Chapter 7

Must I Agonize?

Prayer is measured, not by time, but by intensity. Earnest souls who read of men like Praying Hyde are today anxiously asking, "Am I expected to pray like that?"

They hear of others who sometimes remain on their knees before God all day or all night, refusing food and scorning sleep while they pray and pray and pray. They naturally wonder, "Are we to do the same? Must all of us follow their examples?" We must remember that those men of prayer did not pray by time. They continued so long in prayer because they could not stop praying.

Some have ventured to think that in what has been said in earlier chapters I have hinted that we must all follow in their train. Child of God, do not let any such thought—such fear?—distress you. Just be willing to do what He will have you do, what He leads you to do. Think about it; pray about it. We are bidden by the Lord Jesus to pray to our loving Heavenly Father. We sometimes sing, "Oh, how He loves!" And nothing can fathom that love.

Prayer is not given us as a burden to be borne or an irksome duty to fulfill, but to be a joy and power to which there is no limit. It is given us that we "may find grace to help us in time of need" (Heb. 4:16 RV) And every time is a "time of need." "Pray ye" is an invitation to be accepted rather than a command to be obeyed. Is it a burden for a child to come to his father to ask for some favor? How a father loves his child and seeks its highest good! How he shields that little one from any sorrow or pain or suffering! Our heavenly Father loves us infinitely more than any earthly father. The Lord Jesus loves us infinitely more than any earthly friend. God forgive me if any words of mine, on such a precious theme as prayer, have wounded the hearts or consciences of those who are yearning to know more about prayer. "Your heavenly Father knoweth," said our Lord: and if He knows, we can but trust and not be afraid.

A schoolmaster may blame a boy for neglected homework or unpunctual attendance or frequent absence, but the loving father in the home knows all about it. He knows all about the devoted service of the little laddie in the home circle, where sickness or poverty throws so many loving tasks in his way. Our dear, loving Father knows all about us. He sees. He knows how little leisure some of us have for prolonged periods of prayer.

For some of us God makes leisure. He makes us lie down (Ps. 23:2) that He may make us look up. Even then, weakness of body often prevents prolonged prayer. Yet I question if any of us, however great and reasonable our excuses, spend enough thought over our prayers. Some of us are bound to be much in prayer. Our very work demands it. We may be looked upon as spiritual leaders; we may have responsibility for the spiritual welfare or training of others. God forbid that we should sin against the Lord in ceasing to pray enough for them (1 Sam. 12:23). Yes, with some it is our very business, almost our life's work, to pray. Others

> Have friends who give them pain,
> Yet have not sought a friend in Him.

For them they cannot help praying. If we have the burden of souls upon us we shall never ask, "How long need I pray?"

But how well we know the difficulties that surround the prayer life of many! A little pile of letters lies before me as I write. They are full of excuses and kindly protests and reasonings, it is true. But is that why they are written? No! No! Far from it. In every one of them there is an undercurrent of deep yearning to know God's will and how to obey the call to prayer amid all the countless claims of life.

Those letters tell of many who cannot get away from others for times of secret prayer; of those who share even bedrooms; of busy mothers and maids and mistresses who scarcely know how to get through the endless washing and cooking, mending and cleaning, shopping and visiting; of tired workers who are too weary to pray when the day's work is done.

Child of God, our heavenly Father knows all about it. He is not a taskmaster. He is our Father. If you have no time for prayer or no chance of secret prayer, just tell Him all about it, and you will discover that you are praying!

To those who seem unable to get any solitude at all, or even the opportunity of stealing into a quiet church for a few moments, may we point to the wonderful prayer life of St. Paul? Did it ever occur to you that he was in prison when he wrote most of those marvelous prayers of his that we possess? Picture him. He was chained to a Roman soldier day and night and was never alone for a moment. Epaphras was there part of the time and caught something of his master's passion for prayer. St. Luke may have been there. What prayer meetings! No opportunity for secret prayer. No! but how much we owe to the uplifting of those chained hands! You and I may be never, or rarely ever, alone, but at least our hands are not fettered with chains, and our hearts are not fettered, nor our lips.

Can we make time for prayer? I may be wrong, but my own belief is that it is not God's will for most of us, and perhaps not for any of us, to spend so much time in prayer as to injure our physical health through getting insufficient food or sleep. With very many it is a physical impossibility, because of bodily weakness, to remain long in the spirit of intense prayer.

The posture in which we pray is immaterial. God will listen whether we kneel or stand or sit or walk or work.

I am quite aware that many have testified that God sometimes gives special strength to those who curtail their hours of rest to pray more. At one time the writer tried getting up very early every morning for prayer and communion with God. After a time he found that his daily work was suffering in intensity and effectiveness, and that it was difficult to keep awake during the early evening hours! But do we pray as much as we might do? It is a lasting regret to me that I allowed the days of youth and vigor to pass by without laying more stress upon those early hours of prayer.

Now, the inspired command is clear enough: "Pray without ceasing" (1 Thess. 5:17). Our dear Lord said, "Men ought always to pray, and not to faint . . . and never lose heart" (Luke 18:1 WEYMOUTH).

This, of course, cannot mean that we are to be always on our knees. I am convinced that God does not wish us to neglect rightful work to pray. But it is equally certain that we might work better and do more work if we gave less time to work and more to prayer.

Let us work well. We are to be "not slothful in business" (Rom. 12:11). St. Paul says, "We exhort you, brethren, that ye abound more and more; and that ye . . . do your own business, and to work with your hands . . . that ye may walk honestly . . . and have need of nothing"(1 Thess: 4:11–12). "If any will not work, neither let him eat" (1 Thess. 3:10).

But are there not endless opportunities during every day of "lifting up holy hands"—or at least holy hearts—in prayer to our Father? Do we seize the opportunity, as we open our eyes upon each new day, of praising and blessing our Redeemer? Every day is an Easter day to the Christian. We can pray as we dress. Without a reminder we shall often forget. In the corner of your looking-glass, stick a piece of paper bearing the words, "Pray without ceasing." Try it. We can pray as we go from one duty to another. We can often pray at our work. The washing and the writing, the mending and the minding, the cooking and the cleaning will be done all the better for it.

Do not children, both young and old, work better and play better when some loved one is watching? Will it not help us ever to remember that the Lord Jesus is always with us, watching? Yes, and helping. The very consciousness of His eye upon us will be the consciousness of His power within us.

Do you not think that St. Paul had in his mind this

habitual praying rather than fixed seasons of prayer when he said, "The Lord is at hand"—*i.e.*, is near (WEYMOUTH)? "In nothing be anxious, but in everything, by prayer and supplication, with thanksgiving, let your requests be made known unto God" (Phil. 4:5–6). Does not "in everything" suggest that, as thing after thing befalls us, moment by moment, we should then and there make it a "thing" of prayer and praise to the Lord Who is near? "Why should we limit this "nearness" to the Second Advent?

What a blessed thought: prayer is to a near-God. When our Lord sent His disciples forth to work, He said, "Lo, I am with you always."

Sir Thomas Browne, the celebrated physician, had caught this spirit. He made a vow "to pray in all places where quietness inviteth; in any house, highway or street; and to know no street in this city that may not witness that I have not forgotten God and my Savior in it; and that no town or parish where I have been may not say the like. To take occasion of praying upon the sight of any church which I see as I ride about. To pray daily and particularly for my sick patients, and for all sick people, under whose care soever. And at the entrance into the house of the sick to say, "The peace and mercy of God be upon this house.' After a sermon to make prayer and desire a blessing, and to pray for the minister."

But we question if this habitual communion with our blessed Lord is possible unless we have times, whether long or brief, of definite prayer. And what of these prayer seasons? We have said earlier that prayer is as simple as a little child asking something of its father. Nor would such a remark need any further comment were it not for the existence of the evil one.

There is no doubt whatever that the Devil opposes our approach to God in prayer and does all he can to prevent the prayer of faith. His chief way of hindering us is to try to fill our minds with the thought of our needs, so that they shall not be occupied with thoughts of God, our loving Father, to Whom we pray. He wants us to think more of the gift than of the Giver. The Holy Spirit leads us to pray for a brother. We get as far as "O God, bless my brother," and away go our thoughts to the brother and his affairs and his difficulties, his hopes and his fears, and away goes prayer!

How hard the Devil makes it for us to concentrate our thoughts upon God! This is why we urge people to get a realization of the glory of God and the power of God and the presence of God before offering up any petition. If there were no Devil there would be no difficulty in prayer, but it is the evil one's chief aim to make prayer impossible. That is why most of us find it hard to sympathize with those who profess to condemn what they call "vain repetitions" and "much speaking" in prayer, quoting our Lord's words in His sermon on the mount.

A prominent London vicar said quite recently, "God does not wish us to waste either His time or ours with long prayers. We must be businesslike in our dealings with God and just tell Him plainly and briefly what we want and leave the matter there." But does our friend think that prayer is merely making God acquainted with our needs? If that is all there is in it, why, there is no need of prayer! "For your Father knoweth what things ye have need of before ye ask him," said our Lord when urging the disciples to pray.

We are aware that Christ Himself condemned some "long prayer"(Matt. 23:14). But they were long prayers made "for a pretense," "for a show" (Luke 20:47). Dear praying people, believe me, the Lord would equally condemn many of the "long prayers" made every week in some of our prayer meetings—prayers that kill the prayer meeting and finish up with a plea that God would hear these "feeble breathings" or "unworthy utterings."

But he never condemns long prayers that are sincere. Let us not forget that our Lord sometimes spent long nights in prayer. We are told of one of these—we do not know how frequently they were (Luke 6:12). He would sometimes rise a "great while before day" and depart to a solitary place for prayer (Mark 1:35). The perfect Man spent more time in prayer than we do. It would seem an undoubted fact that with God's saints in all ages nights of prayer with God have been followed by days of power with men.

Nor did our Lord excuse Himself from prayer—as we, in our ignorance, might think He could have done—because of the pressing calls to service and boundless opportunities of usefulness. After one of His busiest days, at a time when his popularity was at its highest, just when everyone sought His company and His counsel, He turned His back upon them all and retired to a mountain to pray (Matt. 14:23).

We are told that once "great multitudes came together to hear Him, and to be healed of their infirmities." Then comes the remark, "But Jesus himself constantly withdrew into the desert, and there prayed" (Luke 5:15–16 WEYMOUTH). Why? Because He knew that prayer was then far more potent than "service."

We say we are too busy to pray. But the busier our Lord was, the more He prayed. Sometimes He had no leisure so much as to eat (Mark 3:20); and sometimes He had no leisure for needed rest and sleep (Mark 6:31). Yet He always took time to pray. If frequent prayers and, at times, long hours of prayer were necessary for our Savior, are they less necessary for us?

I do not write to persuade people to agree with me. That is a very small matter. We only want to know the truth. Spurgeon once said: "There is no need for us to go beating about the bush, and not telling the Lord distinctly what it is that we crave at His hands. Nor will it be seemly for us to make any attempt to use fine language; but let us ask God in the simplest and most direct manner for just the things we want. . . . I believe in business prayers. I mean prayers in which you take to God one of the many promises which He has given us in His Word, and expect it to be fulfilled as certainly as we look for the money to be given us when we go to the bank to cash a check. We should not think of going there, lolling over the counter chattering with the clerks on every conceivable subject except the one thing for which we had gone to the bank, and then coming away without the coin we needed; but we should lay before the clerk the promise to pay the bearer a certain sum, tell him in what form we wished to take the amount, count the cash after him, and then go on our way to attend to other business.

That is just an illustration of the method in which we should draw supplies from the Bank of Heaven." Splendid!

By all means let us be definite in prayer. By all means let us put eloquence aside, if we have any! By all means let us avoid needless "chatter" and come in faith, expecting to receive.

But would the bank clerk pass me the money over the counter so readily if there stood by my side a powerful, evil-countenanced, well-armed ruffian whom he recognized to be a desperate criminal waiting to snatch the money before my weak hands could grasp it? Would he not wait till the ruffian had gone? This is no fanciful picture. The Bible teaches us that, in some way or other, Satan can hinder our prayers and delay the answer. Does not St. Peter urge certain things upon Christians, that their "prayers be not hindered" (1 Peter 3:7)? Our prayers can be hindered. "Then cometh the evil one and snatcheth away that which hath been sown in the heart" (Matt. 13:19 RV).

Scripture gives us one instance (probably only one out of many) where the evil one actually delayed, for three weeks, an answer to prayer. We only mention this to show the need of repeated prayer, persistence in prayer, and also to call attention to the extraordinary power that Satan possesses. We refer to Daniel 10:12–13: "Fear not, Daniel, for from the first day that thou didst set thine heart to understand, and to humble thyself before God, thy words were heard: and I am come for thy word's sake. But the prince of the kingdom of Persia withstood me one and twenty days. But lo, Michael, one of the chief princes, came to help me."

We must not overlook this satanic opposition and hindrance to our prayers. If we were to be content to ask God only once for some promised thing or one we deemed necessary, these chapters would never have been written. Are we never to ask again? For instance, I know that God does not will the death of a sinner. So I come boldly in prayer: "O God, save my friend." Am I never to ask for his conversion again? George Müller prayed daily for sixty years for the conversion of a friend. But what light does the Bible throw upon "businesslike" prayers? Our Lord gave two parables to teach persistence and continuance in prayer. The man who asked three loaves from his friend at midnight received as many as he needed "because of his importunity" (WEYMOUTH), or "shamelessness," as the word literally means (Luke 11:8). The widow who "troubled" the unjust judge with her "continual coming" at last secured redress. Our Lord adds, "And shall not God avenge His elect which cry unto Him day and night, and He is long-suffering over them?" (Luke 18:7 RV)

How delighted our Lord was with the poor Syro-Phoenician woman who would not take refusals or rebuffs for an answer! Because of her continual request He said: "O woman, great is thy faith: be it unto thee even as thou wilt" (Matt. 15:28). Our dear Lord, in His agony in Gethsemane, found it necessary to repeat even His prayer. "And he left them and went away and prayed a third time, saying again the same words" (Matt. 26:44). And we find St. Paul, the apostle of prayer, asking God time after time to remove his thorn in the flesh. "Concerning this thing," says he, "I besought the Lord thrice that it might depart from me" (2 Cor. 12:8).

God cannot always grant our petitions immediately. Sometimes we are not fitted to receive the gift. Sometimes He says "No" to give us something far better. Think, too, of the days when St. Peter was in prison. If your boy was unjustly imprisoned, expecting death at any moment, would you (or could you) be content to pray just once, a "business-like" prayer: "O God, deliver my boy from the hands of these men"? Would you not be very much in prayer and very much in earnest?

This is how the Church prayed for St. Peter. "Long and fervent prayer was offered to God by the Church on his behalf" (Acts 12:5 WEYMOUTH). Bible students will have noticed that the KJV rendering, "without ceasing," reads "earnestly" in the RV. Dr. Torrey points out that neither translation gives the full force of the Greek. The word means literally "stretched-out-ed-ly." It represents the soul on the stretch of earnest and intense desire. Intense prayer was made for St. Peter. The very same word is used of our Lord in Gethsemane: "And being in an agony he prayed more earnestly, and his sweat became as it were great drops of blood falling down upon the ground" (Luke 22:44).

Ah! there was earnestness, even agony in prayer. Now, what about our prayers? Are we called upon to agonize in prayer? Many of God's dear saints say "No!" They think such agonizing in us would reveal great want of faith. Yet most of the experiences that befell our Lord are to be ours. We have been crucified with Christ, and we are risen with Him. Shall there be, with us, no travailing for souls?

Come back to human experience. Can we refrain from agonizing in prayer over dearly beloved children who are living in sin? I question if any believer can have the burden of souls upon him, a passion for souls, and not agonize in prayer.

Can we help crying out, like John Knox, "O God, give me Scotland or I die"? Here again the Bible helps us. Was there no travail of soul and agonizing in prayer when Moses cried out to God, "O, this people have sinned a great sin, and have made gods of gold. Yet now, if thou wilt forgive their sin—; and if not, blot me, I pray thee, out of thy book"? (Exod. 32:32).

Was there no agonizing in prayer when St. Paul said, "I could wish"—("pray," RV marg.)—"that I myself were anathema from Christ for my brethren's sake" (Rom. 9:3)?

We may, at all events, be quite sure that our Lord, Who wept over Jerusalem and Who "offered up prayers and supplications with strong crying and tears" (Heb. 5:7), will not be grieved if He sees us weeping over erring ones. Nay, will it not rather gladden His heart to see us agonizing over the sin that grieves Him? In fact, may not the scarcity of conversions in so many a ministry be due to lack of agonizing in prayer?

We are told that "as soon as Zion travailed she brought forth her children" (Isa. 66:8). Was St. Paul thinking of this passage when he wrote to the Galatians, "My little children, of whom I am again in travail until Christ be formed in you" (Gal. 4:19)? And will not this be true of spiritual children? Oh, how cold our hearts often are! How little we grieve over the lost! And shall we dare to criticize those who agonize over the perishing? God forbid! There is such a thing as wrestling in prayer. Not because God is unwilling to answer but because of the opposition of the "world-rulers of this darkness" (Eph. 6:12 RV).

The very word used for "striving" in prayer means "a contest." The contest is not between God and ourselves. He is at one with us in our desires. The contest is with the evil one. Although he is conquered (1 John 3:8), he desires to thwart our prayers.

"We wrestle not against flesh and blood, but against principalities, against the world rulers of this darkness, against the spiritual hosts of wickedness in the heavenly places" (Eph. 6:12). We, too, are in these "heavenly places in Christ" (Eph. 1:3), and it is only in Christ that we can be victorious. Our wrestling may be a wrestling of our thoughts from thinking Satan's suggestions and keeping them fixed on Christ our Savior—that is, watching as well as praying (Eph. 6:18), "watching unto prayer."

We are comforted by the fact that "the Spirit helpeth our infirmities: for we know not how to pray as we ought" (Rom. 8:26). How does the Spirit "help" us, teach us, if not by example as well as by precept? How does the Spirit "pray"? "The Spirit Himself maketh intercession for us with groanings that cannot be uttered" (Rom. 8:26). Does the Spirit "agonize" in prayer as the Son did in Gethsemane?

If the Spirit prays in us, shall we not share His "groanings" in prayer? And if our agonizing in prayer weakens our body at the time, will angels come to strengthen us, as they did our Lord (Luke 22:43)? We may, perhaps, like Nehemiah, weep and mourn and fast when we pray before God (Heb. 1:4). "But," one asks, "may not a godly sorrow for sin and a yearning desire for the salvation of others induce in us an agonizing that is unnecessary and dishonoring to God?"

May it not reveal a lack of faith in God's promises? Perhaps it may do so. But there is little doubt that St. Paul regarded prayer, at least sometimes, as a conflict (see Rom. 15:30). Writing to the Colossian Christians he says: "I would have you know how greatly I strive for you . . . and for as many as have not seen my face in the flesh; that their hearts may be comforted" (Col. 2:1–2). Undoubtedly he refers to his prayers for them.

Again, he speaks of Epaphras as one who is "always striving for you in his prayers, that ye may stand perfect, and fully assured in all the will of God" (Col. 4:12).

The word for "strive" is our word "agonize," the very word used of our Lord being "in an agony" when praying Himself (Luke 22:44).

The apostle says again, Epaphras "hath much labor for you," that is, in his prayers. St. Paul saw him praying there in prison and witnessed his intense striving as he engaged in a long indefatigable effort on behalf of the Colossians. How the Praetorian guard to whom St. Paul was chained must have wondered (and have been deeply touched) to see these men at their prayers. Their agitation, their tears, their earnest supplications as they lifted up chained hands in prayer must have been a revelation to him! What would they think of our prayers?

No doubt St. Paul was speaking of his own custom when he urged the Ephesian Christians and others "to stand," "with all prayer and supplication, praying at all seasons in the Spirit, and watching thereunto in all perseverance and supplication for all saints, and on my behalf . . . an ambassador in chains" (Eph. 6:18–20). That is a picture of his own prayer life, we may be sure.

So then prayer meets with obstacles that must be prayed away. That is what men mean when they talk about praying through. We must wrestle with the machinations of Satan. It may be bodily weariness or pain or the insistent claims of other thoughts or doubt or the direct assaults of spiritual hosts of wickedness. With us, as with St. Paul, prayer is something of a "conflict," a "wrestle," at least sometimes, which compels us to "stir" ourselves up "to lay hold on God" (Isa. 64:7). Should we be wrong if we ventured to suggest that very few people ever wrestle in prayer? Do we? But let us never doubt our Lord's power and the riches of His grace.

The author of *The Christian's Secret of Happy Life* told a

little circle of friends, just before her death, of an incident in her own life. Perhaps I may be allowed to tell it abroad. A lady friend who occasionally paid her a visit for two or three days was always a great trial, a veritable tax upon her temper and her patience. Every such visit demanded much prayer preparation. The time came when this "critical Christian" planned a visit for a whole week! She felt that nothing but a whole night of prayer could fortify her for this great testing. So, providing herself with a little plate of biscuits, she retired in good time to her bedroom, to spend the night on her knees before God to beseech Him to give her grace to keep sweet and loving during the impending visit. No sooner had she knelt beside her bed than there flashed into her mind the words of Phil. 4:19: "God shall supply all your needs according to His riches in glory by Christ Jesus." Her fears vanished. She said, "When I realized that, I gave Him thanks and praised Him for His goodness. Then I jumped into bed and slept the night through. My guest arrived the next day, and I quite enjoyed her visit."

No one can lay down hard and fast rules of prayer, even for himself. God's gracious Holy Spirit alone can direct us moment by moment. There, however, we must leave the matter. God is our Judge and our Guide. But let us remember that prayer is a many-sided thing. As Bishop Moule says, "True prayer can be uttered under innumerable circumstances." Very often

> Prayer is the burden of a sigh
>   The falling of a tear,
> The upward glancing of an eye
>   When none but God is near.

It may be just letting your request be made known unto God (Phil. 4:6). We cannot think that prayer need always be a conflict and a wrestle. For if it were, many of us would soon become physical wrecks, suffering from nervous break-downs, and coming to early graves.

And with many it is a physical impossibility to stay any length of time in a posture of prayer. Dr. Moule says:

"Prayer, genuine and victorious, is continually offered without the least physical effort or disturbance. It is often in the deepest stillness of soul and body that it wins its longest way. But there is another side of the matter. Prayer is never meant to be indolently easy, however simple and reliant it may be. It is meant to be an infinitely important transaction between man and God. And therefore, very often . . . it has to be viewed as a work involving labor, persistence, conflict, if it would be prayer indeed."

No one can prescribe for another. Let each be persuaded in his own mind how to pray, and the Holy Spirit will inspire us and guide us how long to pray. And let us all be so full of the love of God our Savior that prayer, at all times and in all places, may be a joy as well as a means of grace.

> Shepherd Divine, our wants relieve
> In this and every day;
> To all Thy tempted followers give
> The power to watch and pray.
>
> The spirit of interceding grace
> Give us the faith to claim;
> To wrestle till we see Thy face
> And know Thy hidden Name.

Chapter 8

Does God Always Answer Prayer?

We now come to one of the most important questions that any person can ask. Very much depends upon the answer we are led to give. Let us not shrink from facing the question fairly and honestly. Does God always answer prayer? Of course, we all grant that He does answer prayer—some prayers, sometimes. But does He always answer true prayer? Some so-called prayers He does not answer, because He does not hear them. When His people were rebellious, He said, "When ye make many prayers, I will not hear" (Isa. 1:15).

But a child of God ought to expect answers to prayer. God means every prayer to have an answer. Not a single real prayer can fail of its effect in heaven.

And yet that wonderful declaration of St. Paul, "all things are yours, for ye are Christ's" (1 Cor. 3:21), seems so plainly and so tragically untrue for most Christians. Yet it is not so. They are ours, but so many of us do not possess our possessions. The owners of Mount Morgan, in Queensland, toiled arduously for years on its barren slopes, eking out a miserable existence, never knowing that under their feet was one of the richest sources of gold the world has ever known. There was wealth, vast, undreamt of, yet unimagined and unrealized. It was "theirs," yet not theirs.

The Christian, however, knows of the riches of God in glory in Christ Jesus, but he does not seem to know how to get them.

Now, our Lord tells us that they are to be had for the asking. May He indeed give us all a right judgment in "prayer things." When we say that no true prayer goes unanswered we are not claiming that God always gives just what we ask for. Have you ever met a parent so foolish as to treat his child like that? We do not give our child a red-hot poker because he clamors for it! Wealthy people are the most careful not to allow their children much pocket money.

Why, if God gave us all we prayed for, we should rule the world and not He! And surely we would all confess that we are not capable of doing that. Moreover, more than one ruler of the world is an absolute impossibility!

God's answer to prayer may be "Yes," or it may be "No." It may be "Wait," for it may be that He plans a much larger blessing than we imagined, and one that involves other lives as well as our own.

God's answer is sometimes "No." But this is not necessarily a proof of known and wilful sin in the life of the suppliant, although there may be sins of ignorance. He said "No" to St. Paul sometimes (2 Cor. 12:8–9). More often than not the refusal is due to our ignorance or selfishness in asking. "For we know not how to pray as we ought" (Rom. 8:26). That was what was wrong with the mother of Zebedee's children. She came and worshiped our Lord and prayed to Him. He quickly replied, "Ye know not what ye ask" (Matt. 20:22). Elijah, a great man of prayer, sometimes had "No" for an answer. But when he was swept up to glory in a chariot of fire, did he regret that God said "No" when he cried out "O Lord, take away my life"?

God's answer is sometimes "Wait." He may delay the answer because we are not yet fit to receive the gift we crave, as with wrestling Jacob. Do you remember the famous prayer of Augustine: "O God, make me pure, but not now"? Are not our prayers sometimes like that? Are we always really willing to "drink the cup," to pay the price of answered prayer? Sometimes He delays so that greater glory may be brought to Himself.

God's delays are not denials. We do not know why He sometimes delays the answer and at other times answers "before we call" (Isa. 65:24). George Müller, one of the greatest men of prayer of all time, had to pray over a period of more than sixty-three years for the conversion of a friend! Who can tell why? "The great point is never to give up until the answer comes," said Müller. "I have been praying for sixty-three years and eight months for one man's conversion. He is not converted yet, but he will be! How can it be otherwise? There is the unchanging promise of Jehovah, and on that I rest." Was this delay due to some persistent hindrance from the Devil (Dan. 10:13)? Was it a mighty and prolonged effort on the part of Satan to shake or break Müller's faith? For no sooner was Müller dead than his friend was converted—even before the funeral.

Yes, his prayer was granted, though the answer tarried long in coming. So many of George Müller's petitions were granted him that it is no wonder that he once exclaimed, "Oh, how good, kind, gracious and condescending is the One with Whom we have to do! I am only a poor, frail, sinful man, but He has heard my prayers ten thousands of times."

Perhaps some are asking, How can I discover whether God's answer is "No" or "Wait"? We may rest assured that He will not let us pray sixty-three years to get a "No"! Müller's prayer, so long repeated, was based upon the knowledge that God "willeth not the death of a sinner", "He would have all men to be saved" (1 Tim. 2:4).

Even as I write, the postman brings me an illustration of this. A letter comes from one who very rarely writes me and did not even know my address, one whose name is known to every Christian worker in England. A loved one was stricken down with illness. Is he to continue to pray for her recovery? Is God's answer "No," or is it, "Go on praying and wait"? My friend writes: "I had distinct guidance from God regarding my beloved . . . that it was the will of God she should be taken . . . I retired into the rest of surrender and submission to His will. I have much to praise God for." A few hours later God took that loved one to be with Him in glory.

Again may we urge our readers to hold on to this truth: true prayer never goes unanswered.

If we only gave more thought to our prayers we would pray

more intelligently. That sounds like a truism. But we say it because some dear Christian people seem to lay their common sense and reason aside before they pray. A little reflection would show that God cannot grant some prayers. During the war every nation prayed for victory. Yet it is perfectly obvious that all countries could not be victorious. Two men living together might pray, the one for rain and the other for fine weather. God cannot give both these things at the same time in the same place!

But the truthfulness of God is at stake in this matter of prayer. We have all been reading again those marvelous prayer promises of our Lord and have almost staggered at those promises, the wideness of their scope, the fullness of their intent, the largeness of the one word "Whatsoever." Very well! "Let God be found true" (Rom. 3:4). He certainly will always be "found true."

Do not stop to ask the writer if God has granted all his prayers. He has not. To have said "Yes" to some of them would have spelled curse instead of blessing. To have answered others was, alas, a spiritual impossibility; he was not worthy of the gifts he sought. The granting of some of them would have but fostered spiritual pride and self-satisfaction. How plain all these things seem now, in the fuller light of God's Holy Spirit!

As one looks back and compares one's eager, earnest prayers with one's poor, unworthy service and lack of true spirituality, one sees how impossible it was for God to grant the very things He longed to impart! It was often like asking God to put the ocean of His love into a thimble-heart! And yet, how God just yearns to bless us with every spiritual blessing! How the dear Savior cries again and again, "How often would I . . . but ye would not" (Matt. 23:37). The sadness of it all is that we often ask and do not receive because of our unworthiness, and then we complain because God does not answer our prayers! The Lord Jesus declares that God gives the Holy Spirit, who teaches us how to pray, just as readily as a father gives good gifts to his children. But no gift is a "good gift" if the child is not fit to use that gift. God never gives us something that we cannot or will not use for His glory (I am not referring to talents, for we may abuse or "bury" those, but to spiritual gifts).

Did you ever see a father give his baby boy a razor when he asked for it, because he hoped the boy would grow into a man and then find the razor useful? Does a father never say to his child, "Wait till you are older (or bigger or wiser or better or stronger)"? May not our loving heavenly Father also say to us, "Wait"? In our ignorance and blindness we must surely sometimes say,

> In very love refuse
> Whate'er Thou seest
> Our weakness would abuse.

Rest assured that God never bestows tomorrow's gift today. It is not unwillingness on His part to give. It is not that God is ever straitened in Himself. His resources are infinite, and His ways are past finding out. It was after bidding His disciples to ask that our Lord went on to hint not only at His providence, but at His resources. "Look at the wild birds" (Matt. 6:26 MOFFATT); "your heavenly Father feedeth them." How simple it sounds. Yet have you ever reflected that not a single millionaire, the wide world over, is wealthy enough to feed all "the birds of the air," even for one day? Your heavenly Father feedeth them every day and is none the poorer for it. Shall He not much more feed you, clothe you, take care of you?

Oh, let us rely more upon prayer! Do we not know that "He is a Rewarder of them that diligently seek Him" (Heb. 11:6)? The "oil" of the Holy Spirit will never cease to flow so long as there are empty vessels to receive it (1 Kings 4:6). It is always we who are to blame when the Spirit's work ceases. God cannot trust some Christians with the fullness of the Holy Spirit. God cannot trust some workers with definite spiritual results in their labors. They would suffer from pride and vainglory. No! We do not claim that God grants every Christian everything he prays for.

As we saw in an earlier chapter, there must be purity of heart, purity of motive, purity of desire, if our prayers are to be in His name. God is greater than His promises and often gives more than either we desire or deserve, but He does not always do so. So, then, if any specific petition is not granted, we may feel sure that God is calling us to examine our hearts. For He has undertaken to grant every prayer that is truly offered in His name. Let us repeat His blessed words once more—we cannot repeat them too often— "Whatsoever ye shall ask in My name, that will I do, that the Father may be glorified in the Son. If ye shall ask anything in My name, that will I do" (John 14:13–14).

Remember that is was impossible for Christ to offer up any prayer that was not granted. He was God. He knew the mind of God. He had the mind of the Holy Spirit.

Does He once say, "Father, if it be possible, let . . ." as He kneels in agony in Gethsemane's garden, pouring out strong crying and tears? Yes, and "He was heard for His reverential awe" (Heb. 5:7 MOULE). Surely not the "agony," but the sonlike fear, gained the answer? Our prayers are heard not so much because they are important but because they are filial.

Fellow Christian, we cannot fully understand that hallowed scene of dreadful awe and wonder. But this we know: our Lord never yet made a promise that He cannot keep or does not mean to fulfill. The Holy Spirit maketh intercession for us (Rom. 8:26), and God cannot say Him "Nay." The Lord Jesus makes intercession for us (Heb. 7:25), and God cannot say Him "Nay." His prayers are worth a thousand of ours, but it is He who bids us pray!

"But was not St. Paul filled with the Holy Spirit?" you ask. "And did he not say, 'We have the mind of Christ?' Yet he asked thrice over that God would remove the 'thorn' in his flesh, and yet God distinctly told him He would not do so."

It is a very singular thing, too, that the only petition recorded of St. Paul seeking something for his own individual need was refused! The difficulty, however, is this: Why did St. Paul, who had the "mind" of Christ, ask for something that he soon discovered was contrary to God's wishes? There are doubtless many fully consecrated Christians reading these words who have been perplexed because God has not given some things they prayed for.

We must remember that we may be filled with the Spirit and yet err in judgment or desire. We must remember, too, that we are never filled with God's Holy Spirit once and for all. The evil one is always on the watch to put his mind into us, so as to strike at God through us. At any moment we may become disobedient or unbelieving, or may be betrayed into some thought or act contrary to the Spirit of love.

We have an astonishing example of this in the life of St. Peter. At one moment, under the compelling influence of God's Holy Spirit, he cries, "Thou art the Christ, the Son of the living God!" Our Lord turns and with words of high commendation says, "Blessed art thou, Simon, for flesh and blood hath not revealed it unto thee, but My Father, which is in heaven." Yet a very little while after, the Devil gets his mind into St. Peter, and our Lord turns and says unto him, "Get thee behind me, Satan!" (Matt. 16:17, 23). St. Peter was now speaking in the name of Satan. Satan still "desires to have" us.

St. Paul was tempted to think that he could do far better work for his beloved Master if only that "thorn" could be removed. But God knew that Paul would be a better man with the "thorn" than without it.

Is it not a comfort to us to know that we may bring more glory to God under something that we are apt to regard as a hindrance or handicap, than if that undesired thing was removed? "My grace is sufficient for thee: My power is made perfect in weakness" (2 Cor. 12:9). Remember that

> God nothing does, nor suffers to be done,
> But what thou would'st thyself
> Did'st thou but see
> The end of all He does as well as He.

St. Paul was not infallible, nor were St. Peter or St. John; nor is the Pope or any other man. We may—and do—offer up mistaken prayers. The highest form of prayer is not, "Thy way, O God, not mine," but "My way, O God, is Thine!" We are taught to pray, not "Thy will be changed," but "Thy will be done."

May we, in conclusion, give the testimony of two who have proved that God can be trusted?

Sir H. M. Stanley, the great explorer, wrote: "I for one must not dare to say that prayers are inefficacious. Where I have been in earnest, I have been answered. Where I prayed for light to guide my followers wisely through the perils that beset them, a ray of light has come upon the perplexed mind, and a clear road to deliverance has been pointed out. You may know when prayer is answered, by the glow of content that fills one who has flung his cause before God, as he rises to his feet. I have evidence, satisfactory to myself, that prayers are granted."

Mary Slessor, the story of whose life in West Africa has surely thrilled us all, was once asked what prayer meant to her. She replied, "My life is one long, daily, hourly record of answered prayer for physical health, for mental overstrain, for guidance given marvelously, for errors and dangers averted, for enmity to the Gospel subdued, for food provided at the exact hour needed, for everything that goes to make up life and my poor service. I can testify with a full and often wonder-stricken awe that I believe God answers prayer. I know God answers prayer!"

Chapter 9

Answers to Prayer

Mere human nature would choose a more startling title to this chapter: remarkable answers; wonderful answers; amazing answers. But we must allow God to teach us that it is as natural to Him to answer prayer as it is for us to ask. How He delights to hear our petitions, and how He loves to answer them! When we hear of some wealthy person giving a treat to poverty-stricken people or wiping out some crushing deficit in a missionary society, we exclaim, "How nice to be able to do a thing like that!" Well, if it is true that God loves us (and we know it is true), do you not think it gives Him great joy to give us what we ask? We should like, therefore, to recount one or two answers to prayer out of very many that have come to our notice, so that we may have greater boldness in coming to the Throne of Grace. God saves men for whom we pray. Try it.

In talking over this question with a man of prayer a few days ago, he suddenly asked me, "Do you know St. M——'s Church L——?"

"Quite well. I've been there several times."

"Let me tell you what happened when I lived there. We had a prayer meeting each Sunday before the 8 o'clock communion service. As we rose from our knees one Sunday a sidesman said, 'Vicar, I wish you would pray for my boy. He is twenty-two years old now and has not been to church for years.' 'We can spare five minutes now,' replied the vicar.

They knelt down again and offered up earnest supplication on behalf of that man. Although nothing was said to him about this, that youth came to church that same evening. Something in the sermon convicted him of sin. He came into the vestry, broken-hearted, and accepted Jesus Christ as his Savior."

On Monday morning my friend, who was working as a Church Army captain in the parish, was present at the weekly meeting of the staff. He said to the vicar, "That conversion last night is a challenge to prayer—a challenge from God. Shall we accept it?" "What do you mean?" asked the vicar. "Well," said he, "shall we single out the worst man in the parish and pray for him?" By unanimous consent they fixed upon K—— as the worst man they knew. So they "agreed" in prayer for his conversion. At the end of that week, as they were conducting a Saturday night prayer meeting in the mission hall, and while his very name was on their lips, the door swung open and in staggered K——, much the worse for liquor. He had never been in that mission hall before. Without thinking of removing his cap he sank on a chair near the door and buried his face in his hands. The prayer meeting suddenly became an enquiry-room. Even as he was, he sought the Lord Who was seeking him. Nor did he ever go back. Today he is one of the finest dockyard missioners in the land.

Oh, why do we not pray for our unconverted friends? They may not listen to us when we plead with them, but they cannot hold out if we pray for them. Let two or three agree in prayer over the salvation of the worst and then see what God will do! Tell God and then trust God. God works in a wonderful way, as well as in a "mysterious" way, His wonders to perform.

Dan Crawford told us recently that when returning to his mission field after a furlough, it was necessary to make all possible haste. But a deep stream, which had to be crossed, was in flood, and no boats were available, or usable for that matter. So he and his party camped and prayed. An infidel might well have laughed aloud. How could God get them across that river! But as they prayed, a tall tree, which had battled with that river for scores of years, began to totter and fall. It fell clear across the stream! As Mr. Crawford says, "The Royal Engineers of heaven had laid a pontoon bridge for God's servants."

Many young people will be reading these prayer stories. May we remind them that God still hears the voice of the lad and the lass (Gen. 21:17)? For them may we be allowed to add the following story, with the earnest desire that prayer may be their heritage, their very life; and that answered prayer may be their daily experience.

Some little time ago, a Chinese boy of twelve years old, named Ma-Na-Si, a boarder in the mission school at Chefoo, went home for the holidays. He is the son of a native pastor.

While standing on the doorstep of his father's house, he espied a horseman galloping toward him. The man, a heathen, was in a great state of perturbation. He eagerly enquired for the "Jesus-man"—the pastor. The boy told him that his father was away from home. The poor man was much distressed and hurriedly explained the cause of his visit. He had been sent from a heathen village some miles away to fetch the "holy man" to cast a devil out of the daughter-in-law of a heathen friend. He poured out his sad story of this young woman, torn by devils, raving and reviling, pulling out her hair, clawing her face, tearing her clothes, smashing up furniture, and dashing away dishes of food. He told of her spirit of sacrilege, outrageous impiety, and brazen blasphemy, and how these outbursts were followed by foaming at the mouth and great exhaustion, both physical and mental. "But my father is not at home," the boy kept reiterating. At length the frenzied man seemed to understand. Suddenly he fell on his knees and, stretching out his hands in desperation, cried, "You, too, are a Jesus-man; will you come?"

Think of it! A boy of twelve! Yes, but even a lad, when fully yielded to his Savior, is not fearful of being used by that Savior. There was but one moment of surprise, and a moment of hesitation, and then the laddie put himself wholly at his Master's disposal. Like little Samuel of old he was willing to obey God in all things. He accepted the earnest entreaty as a call from God. The heathen stranger sprang into the saddle, and swinging the Christian boy up behind him, he galloped away.

Ma-Na-Si began to think over things. He had accepted an invitation to cast out a devil in the name of Christ Jesus. But was he worthy to be used of God in this way? Was his heart pure and his faith strong? As they galloped along he carefully searched his own heart for sin to be confessed and repented of. Then he prayed for guidance in what to say and how to act, and tried to recall Bible instances of demoniacal possession and how they were dealt with. Then he simply and humbly cast himself upon the God of power and of mercy, asking His help for the glory of the Lord Jesus. On arrival at the house they found that some of the members of the family were by main force holding down the tortured woman upon the bed. She had not been told that a messenger had gone for the native pastor, yet as soon as she heard footsteps in the court outside, she cried, "All of you get out of my way; a man is coming. I cannot endure him. His name is Ma-Na-Si."

Ma-Na-Si entered the room and after a ceremonial bow knelt down and began to pray. Then he sang a Christian hymn to the praise of the Lord Jesus. Then, in the name of the Risen Lord, glorified and omnipotent, he commanded the demon to come out of the woman. At once she was calm, though prostrate with weakness. From that day she was perfectly whole. She was amazed when they told her that she had uttered the name of the Christian boy, for she had never heard of it or read of it before, for the whole of that village was heathen. But that day was veritably a "beginning of days" to those people, for from it the Word of the Lord had free course and was glorified.

Beloved reader, I do not know how this little narrative affects you. It is one that moves me to the very depths of my being. It seems to me that most of us know so little of the power of God, so little of His overwhelming, irresistible love. Oh, what love is His! Now, every time we pray, that wonderful love envelops us in a special way.

If we really loved our blessed Savior, should we not oftener seek communion with Him in prayer? Fellow Christian, is it because we pray so little that we criticize so much? Oh, let us remember that we, like our dear Savior, are not sent into the world to condemn, to judge, the world, "but that the world should be saved through Him (John 3:17).

Will any thoughtless word of criticism of anyone move anyone nearer to Christ? Will it even help the utterer of that fault-finding to be more like the Master? Oh, let us lay aside the spirit of criticism, of blaming, of fault-finding, of disparaging others or their work. Would not St. Paul say to us all, "And such were some of you, but ye are washed" (2 Cor. 6:11)?

Do you see what we are aiming at? All the evil dispositions and failings we detect in others are due to the Devil. It is the evil one in the heart who causes those words and deeds that we are so ready to condemn and to exaggerate. Demon-possession is not unknown in England, but it takes a different form, perhaps. Our very friends and acquaintances, so kindly and lovable, are often tied and bound by some besetting sin—"whom Satan hath bound, lo, these many years."

We may plead with them in vain. We may warn them in vain. Courtesy and charity, and our own failings and shortcomings, forbid us standing over them like Ma-Na-Si and exorcising the evil spirit! But have we tried prayer— prayer always backed up by love that "cannot be provoked" (1 Cor. 13:5)?

God answers prayer from old and young when there is a clean heart, a holy life, and a simple faith. God answers prayer. We are but frail and faulty servants at the best. Sincere as we may be, we shall sometimes ask amiss. But God is faithful that promised, and He will guard us from all harm and supply every need.

> Can I have the things I pray for?
>   God knows best;
> He is wiser than His children.
>   I can rest.

"Beloved, if our heart condemn us not, we have boldness toward God; and whatsoever we ask we receive of him, because we keep his commandments, and do those things that are pleasing in his sight" (1 John 3:21).

Chapter 10

How God Answers Prayers

For man fully to understand God and all His dealings with us is an utter impossibility. "O the depth of the riches both of the wisdom and the knowledge of God! How unsearchable are his judgments, and his ways past tracing out!" (Rom. 11:33). True, but we need not make difficulties where none exist. If God has all power and all knowledge, surely prayer has no difficulties, though occasionally there may be perplexities. We cannot discover God's method, but we know something of His manner of answering prayer.

But at the very outset may we remind ourselves how little we know about ordinary things? Mr. Edison, whose knowledge is pretty profound, wrote in August, 1921, "We don't know the millionth part of one per cent about anything. We don't know what water is. We don't know what light is. We don't know what gravitation is. We don't know what enables us to keep on our feet to stand up. We don't know what electricity is. We don't know what heat is. We don't know anything about magnetism. We have a lot of hypotheses, but that is all." But we do not allow our ignorance about all these things to deprive us of their use! We do not know much about prayer, but surely this need not prevent us from praying! We do know what our Lord has taught us about prayer. And we do know that He has sent the Holy Spirit to teach us all things (John 14:26). How, then, does God answer prayer?

He reveals His mind to those who pray. His Holy Spirit puts fresh ideas into the minds of praying people. We are quite aware that the Devil and his angels are busy enough putting bad thoughts into our minds. Surely, then, God and His holy angels can give us good thoughts? Even poor, weak, sinful men and women can put good thoughts into the minds of others. That is what we try to do in writing! We do not stop to think what a wonderful thing it is that a few peculiarly shaped black marks on this white paper can uplift and inspire or depress and cast down or even convict of sin! But, to an untutored savage, it is a stupendous miracle. Moreover, you and I can often read people's thoughts or wishes from an expression on the face or a glance of the eye. Even thought transference between man and man is a commonplace today. And God can in many ways convey His thoughts to us. A remarkable instance of this was related by a speaker last year at Northfield. Three or four years ago, he met an old whaling captain who told him this story.

"A good many years ago, I was sailing in the desolate seas off Cape Horn, where I was hunting whales. One day we were beating directly south in the face of a hard wind. We had been tacking this way and that all morning and were making very little headway. About 11 o'clock, as I stood at the wheel, the idea suddenly came into my mind, 'Why batter the ship against those waves? There are probably as many whales to the north as to the south. Suppose we run with the wind instead of against it?' In response to that sudden idea, I changed the course of the ship and began to sail north instead of south. One hour later, at noon, the look-out at the masthead shouted 'Boats ahead!' Presently we overtook four lifeboats, in which were fourteen sailors, the only survivors of the crew of a ship that had burned to the water's edge ten days before. Those men had been adrift in their boats ever since, praying God frantically for rescue, and we arrived just in time to save them. They could not have survived another day."

Then the old whaler added, "I don't know whether you believe in religion or not, but I happen to be a Christian. I have begun every day of my life with prayer that God would use me to help someone else, and I am convinced that God, that day, put the idea into my mind to change the course of my ship. That idea saved fourteen lives."

God has many things to say to us. He has many thoughts to put into our minds. We are apt to be so busy doing His work that we do not stop to listen to His Word. Prayer gives God the opportunity of speaking to us and revealing His will to us. May our attitude often be: "Speak, Lord, Thy servant heareth."

God answers other prayers by putting new thoughts into the minds of those we pray for. At a series of services dealing with the Victorious Life, the writer one afternoon urged the congregation to "make up" their quarrels if they really desired a holy life. One lady went straight home and after very earnest prayer wrote to her sister, with whom, owing to some disagreement, she had had nothing to do for twenty years! Her sister was living thirty miles away. The very next morning the writer of that note received a letter from that very sister asking forgiveness and seeking reconciliation. The two letters had crossed in the post. While the one sister was praying to God for the other, God was speaking to that other sister, putting into her mind the desire for reconciliation.

You may say, Why did not God put that desire there before? It may be that He foresaw that it would be useless for the distant sister to write asking forgiveness until the other sister was also willing to forgive. The fact remains that, when we pray for others, somehow or other it opens the way for God to influence those we pray for. God needs our prayers, or He would not beg us to pray.

A little time back, at the end of a weekly prayer meeting, a godly woman begged those present to pray for her husband, who would never go near a place of worship. The leader suggested that they should continue in prayer then and there. Most earnest prayers were offered up. Now, the husband was devoted to his wife and frequently came to meet her. He did so that night and arrived at the hall while the prayer meeting was still in progress. God put it into his mind to open the door and wait inside, a thing he had never done before. As he sat on a chair near the door, leaning his head upon his hand, he overheard those earnest petitions. During the homeward walk he said, "Wife, who was the man they were praying for tonight?" "Oh," she replied, "It is the husband of one of our workers." "Well, I am quite sure he will be saved," he said: "God must answer prayers like that." A little later in the evening he again asked, "Who was the man they were praying for?" She replied in similar terms as before. On retiring to rest he could not sleep. He was under deep conviction of sin. Awaking his wife, he begged her to pray for him.

How clearly this shows us that when we pray, God can work! God could have prompted that man to enter that prayer meeting any week. But had he done so it is a question whether any good at all would have come from it. When once those earnest, heart-felt petitions were being offered up on his behalf God saw that they would have a mighty influence upon that poor man.

It is when we pray that God can help us in our work and strengthen our resolves. For we can answer many of our own prayers. One bitter winter a prosperous farmer was praying that God would keep a neighbor from starving. When the family prayers were over, his little boy said, "Father, I don't think I should have troubled God about that." "Why not?" he asked. "Because it would be easy enough for you to see that they don't starve!" There is not the slightest doubt that if we pray for others we shall also try to help them.

A young convert asked his vicar to give him some Christian work. "Have you a chum?" "Yes," replied the boy. "Is he a Christian?" "No, he is as careless as I was." "Then go and ask him to accept Christ as his Savior." "Oh, no!" said the lad, "I could never do that. Give me anything but that." "Well," said the vicar, "promise me two things: that you will not speak to him about his soul, and that you will pray to God twice daily for his conversion." "Why, yes, I'll gladly do that," answered the boy. Before a fortnight was up he rushed round to the vicarage. "Will you let me off my promise? I must speak to my chum!" he cried. When he began to pray, God could give him strength to witness. Communion with God is essential before we can have real communion with our fellow man. My belief is that men so seldom speak to others about their spiritual condition because they pray so little for them.

The writer has never forgotten how his faith in prayer was confirmed when, as a lad of thirteen, he earnestly asked God to enable him on a certain day to secure twenty new subscribers for missions overseas. Exactly twenty new names were secured before night closed in. The consciousness that God would grant that prayer was an incentive to eager effort and gave an unwonted courage in approaching others.

A cleric in England suggested to his people that they should each day pray for the worst man or woman and then go to them and tell them about Jesus. Only six agreed to do so. On arrival home he began to pray. Then he said, "I must not leave this to my people. I must take it up myself. I don't know the bad people. I'll have to go out and enquire." Approaching a rough-looking man at a street corner, he asked, "Are you the worst man in this district?" "No, I'm not." "Would you mind telling me who is?" "I don't mind. You'll find him at No. 7, down that street."

He knocked at No. 7 and entered. "I'm looking for the worst man in my parish. They tell me it might be you?" "Whoever told you that? Fetch him here, and I'll show him who's the worst man! No, there are lots worse than me." "Well, who is the worst man you know?" "Everybody knows him. He lives at the end house in that court. He's the worst man." So down the court he went and knocked at the door. A surly voice cried, "Come in!"

There was a man and his wife. "I hope you'll excuse me, but I'm the minister of the chapel along the round. I'm looking for the worst man in my district, because I have something to tell him. Are you the worst man?" The man turned to his wife and said, "Lass, tell him what I said to you five minutes ago" "No, tell him yourself." "What were you saying?" enquired the visitor. "Well, I've been drinking for twelve weeks. I've had the D.T.'s and have pawned all in the house worth pawning. And I said to my wife a few minutes ago, 'Lass, this thing has to stop, and if it doesn't, I'll stop it myself—I'll go and drown myself.' Then you knocked at the door! Yes, sir, I'm the very worst man. What have you got to say to me?" "I'm here to tell you that Jesus Christ is the greatest Savior, and that He can make out of the worst man one of the best. He did it for me, and He will do it for you." "D'you think He can do it even for me?" "I'm sure He can. Kneel down and ask Him."

Not only was the poor drunkard saved from his sins, but he is today a radiant Christian man, bringing other drunken people to the Lord Jesus Christ.

Surely none of us finds it difficult to believe that God can, in answer to prayer, heal the body, send rain or fair weather, dispel fogs, or avert calamities?

We have to do with a God whose knowledge is infinite. He can put it into the mind of a doctor to prescribe a certain medicine or diet or method of cure. All the doctor's skill is from God. "He knoweth our frame," for He made it. He knows it far better than the cleverest doctor or surgeon. He made, and He can restore. We believe that God desires us to use medical skill, but we also believe that God, by His wonderful knowledge, can heal, and sometimes does heal, without human cooperation. And God must be allowed to work in His own way. We are so apt to tie God down to meet our approval. God's aim is to glorify His name in answering our prayers. Sometimes He sees that our desire is right but our petition wrong. St. Paul thought he could bring more glory to God if only the thorn in the flesh could be removed. God knew that he would be a better man and do better work with the thorn than without it. So God said, "No, no, no" to his prayer and then explained why!

So it was with Monica, who prayed so many years for the conversion of Augustine, her licentious son. When he was determined to leave home and cross the seas to Rome, she prayed earnestly, even passionately, that God would keep him by her side and under her influence. She went down to a little chapel on the seashore to spend the night in prayer close by where the ship lay at anchor. But, when morning came, she found that the ship had sailed even while she prayed! Her petition was refused, but her real desire was granted. For it was in Rome that Augustine met the sainted Ambrose, who led him to Christ. How comforting it is to know that God knows what is best!

But we should never think it unreasonable that God should make some things dependent upon our prayers. Some people say that if God really loves us He would give us what is best for us whether we ask Him or not. Dr. Fosdick has so beautifully pointed out that God has left man many things to do for himself. He promises seedtime and harvest. Yet man must prepare the soil, sow and till, and reap to allow God to do His share. God provides us with food and drink. There are some things God cannot, or at least will not, do without our help. God cannot do some things unless we think. He never emblazons His truth upon the sky. The laws of science have always been there. But we must think and experiment and think again if we would use those laws for our own good and God's glory.

God cannot do some things unless we work. He stores the hills with marble, but He has never built a cathedral. He fills the mountains with iron ore, but He never makes a needle or a locomotive. He leaves that to us. We must work.

If, then, God has left many things dependent upon humanity's thinking and working, why should He not leave some things dependent upon humanity's praying? He has done so. "Ask and ye shall receive." And there are some things God will not give us unless we ask. Prayer is one of the three ways in which man can cooperate with God, and the greatest of these is prayer.

People of power are without exception people of prayer. God bestows His Holy Spirit in His fullness only on people of prayer. And it is through the operation of the Spirit that answers to prayer come. Every believer has the Spirit of Christ dwelling in him. For "if any have not the Spirit of Christ, he is none of his." But a person of prevailing prayer must be filled with the Spirit of God.

A lady missionary wrote recently that it used to be said of

Praying Hyde that he never spoke to an unconverted man but that he was soundly converted. But if he ever did fail at first to touch a heart for God, he went back to his room and wrestled in prayer till he was shown what it was in himself that had hindered his being used by God. Yes, when we are filled with the Spirit of God, we cannot help influencing others God-ward. But to have power with men we must have power with God.

The momentous question for you and me is not, however, "How does God answer prayer?" The question is, "Do I really pray?" What a marvelous power God places at our disposal! Do we for a moment think that anything displeasing to God is worth our while holding on to? Fellow Christian, trust Christ wholly, and you will find Him wholly true.

Chapter 11

Hindrances to Prayer

The poet said, and we often sing:

> What various hindrances we meet
> In coming to the mercy-seat.

Yes, indeed, they are various. But here again, most of those hindrances are of our own making.

God wants me to pray. The Devil does not want me to pray and does all he can to hinder me. He knows that we can accomplish more through our prayers than through our work. He would rather have us do anything else than pray.

We have already referred to Satan's opposition to prayer:

> Angels our march oppose
>   Who still in strength excel
> Our secret, sworn, relentless foes,
>   Countless, invisible.

But we need not fear them, nor heed them, if our eyes are ever unto the Lord. The holy angels are stronger than fallen angels, and we can leave the celestial hosts to guard us. We believe that to them—the hosts of evil—we owe those wandering thoughts that so often wreck prayer. We no sooner kneel than we "recollect" something that should have been done or something that had better be seen to at once.

These thoughts come from without and are surely due to the promptings of evil spirits. The only cure for wandering thoughts is to get our minds fixed upon God. Undoubtedly a man's worst foe is himself. Prayer is for a child of God, and one who is living as a child of God should pray.

The great question is: Am I harboring any foes in my heart? Are there traitors within? God cannot give us His best spiritual blessings unless we fulfill conditions of trust, obedience, and service. Do we not often ask earnestly for the highest spiritual gifts, without even any thought of fulfilling the necessary requirements? Do we not often ask for blessings we are not fitted to receive? Dare we be honest with ourselves, alone in the presence of God? Dare we say sincerely, "Search me, O God, and see"? Is there anything in me that is hindering God's blessing for me and through me? We discuss the "problem of prayer." We are the problem that needs discussing or dissecting! Prayer is all right! There is no problem in prayer to the heart that is absolutely stayed on Christ.

Now, we shall not quote the usual Bible texts that show how prayer may be frustrated. We merely desire that everyone should get a glimpse of his own heart. No sin is too small to hinder prayer and perhaps to turn the very prayer itself into sin, if we are not willing to renounce that sin. The Moslems in West Africa have a saying: "If there is no purity, there is no prayer; if there is no prayer, there is no drinking of the water of heaven." The truth is so clearly taught in the Scripture that it is amazing that any should try to retain both sin and prayer. Yet very many do this. Even David cried, long ages ago, "If I regard iniquity in my heart, the Lord will not hear" (Ps. 66:18).

And Isaiah says, "Your iniquities have separated between you and your God, and your sins have hid His face from you" (Isa. 59:2). Surely we must all agree that it is sin in us, and not the unwillingness of Christ to hear, that hinders prayer. As a rule, it is some little sin, so-called, that mars and spoils the prayer life. There may be:

(1) Doubt. Now, unbelief is possibly the greatest hindrance to prayer. Our Lord said that the Holy Spirit would convict the world of sin— "of sin because they believe not on Me" (John 16:9). We are not "of the world," yet is there not

much practical unbelief in any of us? St. James, writing to believers, says: "Ask in faith, nothing doubting; for he that doubteth ... let not that man think he shall receive anything of the Lord" (James 1:6–8). Some have not because they ask not. Others "have not" because they believe not. Did you think it a little strange that we spent so much time over adoration and thanksgiving before we came to the "asking"? But surely, if we get a glimpse of the glorious majesty of our Lord and the wonders of His love and grace, unbelief and doubt will vanish away as mists before the rising sun? Was this not the reason that Abraham "staggered not," "wavered not through unbelief," in that he gave God the glory due unto His name, and was therefore "fully assured that what He had promised He was able also to perform" (Rom. 4:20–21)? Knowing what we do of God's stupendous love, is it not amazing that we should ever doubt?

(2) Then there is Self—the root of all sin. How selfish we are prone to be even in our "good works"! How we hesitate to give up anything that "self" craves for. Yet we know that a full hand cannot take Christ's gifts. Was this why the Savior, in the prayer He first taught, coupled us with everything else? "Our" is the first word. "Our Father . . . give us . . . forgive us . . . deliver us. . . ."

Pride prevents prayer, for prayer is a very humbling thing. How hateful pride must be in the sight of God! It is God who gives us all things "richly to enjoy." "What hast thou that thou didst not receive?" asks St. Paul (1 Cor. 4:7). Surely, surely we are not going to let pride, with its hateful, ugly sister, jealousy, ruin our prayer life? God cannot do great things for us whereby we may be glad if they are going to "turn our heads." Oh, how foolish we can be! Sometimes, when we are insistent, God does give us what we ask, at the expense of our holiness. "He gave them their request, but sent leanness into their soul (Ps. 106:15). O God, save us from that—save us from self! Again, self asserts itself in criticizing others. Let this thought burn itself into your memory: The more like Jesus Christ a man becomes, the less he judges other people. It is an infallible test. Those who are always criticizing others have drifted away from Christ. They may still be His, but they have lost His Spirit of love. Beloved reader, if you have a criticizing nature, allow it to dissect yourself and never your neighbor. You will be able to give it full scope, and it will never be unemployed! Is this a harsh remark? Does it betray a tendency to commit the very sin—for it *is* sin—it condemns? It would do so were it spoken to any one individual. But its object is to pierce armor that is seemingly invulnerable. And no one who, for one month, has kept his tongue "from picking and stealing" the reputation of other people will ever desire to go back again to back-biting. "Love suffereth long and is kind" (1 Cor. 13:4). Do we? Are we?

We are ourselves no better because we have managed to paint other people in worse colors than ourselves. But, singularly enough, we enhance our own spiritual joy and our own living witness for Christ when we refuse to pass on disparaging information about others or when we refrain from "judging" the work or lives of other people. It may be hard at first, but it soon brings untold joy and is rewarded by the love of all around. It is most hard to keep silent in the face of "modern" heresies. Are we not told to "contend earnestly for the faith which was once for all delivered unto the saints" (Jude 3)? Sometimes we must speak out, but let it always be in the spirit of love. "Rather let error live than love die."

Even in our private prayers, fault-finding of others must be resolutely avoided. Read once more the story of John Hyde praying for the "cold brother." Believe me, a criticizing spirit destroys holiness of life more easily than anything else because it is such an eminently respectable sin and makes such easy victims of us. We need scarcely add that when a believer is filled with the Spirit of Christ, Who is Love, he will never tell others of the un-Christian behavior he may discern in his friends. "He was most rude to me"; "He is too conceited"; "I can't stand that man"; and such-like remarks are surely unkind, unnecessary, and often untrue.

Our dear Lord suffered the contradiction of sinners against Himself, but He never complained or published abroad the news to others. Why should we do so? Self must be dethroned if Christ is to reign supreme. There must be no idols in the heart. Do you remember what God said of some leaders of religion? "These men have taken their idols into their heart . . .; should I be inquired of at all by them?" (Ezek. 14:3).

When our aim is solely the glory of God, then God can answer our prayers. Christ Himself rather than His gifts should be our desire. "Delight thyself in the Lord and He shall give thee the petitions of thine heart" (Ps. 37:4 RV marg.).

"Beloved, if our heart condemn us not, we have boldness toward God; and whatsoever we ask we receive of Him, because we keep His commandments and do the things that are pleasing in His sight" (1 John 3:21–22).

It is as true today as in the early days of Christianity that men ask and receive not because they ask amiss that they may spend it on their pleasures—*i.e.*, self (James 4:3).

(3) Unlove in the heart is possibly the greatest hindrance to prayer. A loving spirit is a condition of believing prayer. We cannot be wrong with man and right with God. The spirit of prayer is essentially the spirit of love. Intercession is simply love at prayer.

> He prayeth best who loveth best
> All things both great and small;
> For the great God Who loveth us,
> He made and loveth all.

Dare we hate or dislike those whom God loves? If we do, can we really possess the Spirit of Christ? We really must face these elementary facts in our faith if prayer is to be anything more than a mere form. Our Lord not only says, "And pray for those that persecute you; that ye may be sons of your Father Who is in heaven" (Matt. 5:44–45).

We venture to think that large numbers of so-called Christians have never faced this question. To hear how many Christian workers (prominent ones, too) speak of others with whom they disagree, one must charitably suppose they have never heard that command of our Lord!

Our daily life in the world is the best indication of our power in prayer. God deals with my prayers not according to the spirit and tone that I exhibit when I am praying in public or private, but according to the spirit I show in my daily life.

Hot-tempered people can make only frigid prayers. If we do not obey our Lord's command and love one another, our prayers are wellnigh worthless. If we harbor an unforgiving spirit it is almost wasted time to pray. Yet a prominent Dean of one of our cathedrals was recently reported to have said that there are some people we can never forgive! If so, we trust that he uses an abridged form of the Lord's prayer. Christ taught us to say "Forgive us . . . as we forgive." And He goes farther than this. He declares, "If ye forgive not men their trespasses, neither will your heavenly Father forgive your trespasses" (Matt. 6:15). May we ever exhibit the Spirit of Christ and not forfeit our own much-needed forgiveness. How many of our readers who have not the slightest intention of forgiving their enemies, or even their offending friends, repeated the Lord's prayer today?

Many Christians have never given prayer a fair chance. It is not through conscious insincerity, but from want of thought. The blame for it really rests upon those of us who preach and teach. We are prone to teach doctrines rather than doings. Most men desire to do what is right, but they regard the big things rather than the little failings in the life of love.

Our Lord goes so far as to say that even our gifts are not to be presented to God if we remember that our brother "hath ought against us" (Matt. 5:23). If He will not accept our gifts, is it likely He will answer our prayers? It was when Job ceased contending with his enemies (whom the Bible calls his "friends") that the Lord "turned his captivity" and gave him twice as much as he had before (Job 42:10).

How slow we are—how unwilling we are—to see that our lives hinder our prayers! And how unwilling we are to act on love-lines. Yes, we desire to "win" men. Our Lord shows us one way. Don't publish abroad his wrongdoings. Speak to him alone, and "thou hast gained thy brother" (Matt. 18:15). Most of us have rather pained our brothers!

Even the home-life may hinder the prayer life. See what Peter says about how we should so live in the home that our "prayers be not hindered" (1 Peter 3:1—10). We would venture to urge every reader to ask God to search his heart once again and to show him if there is "any root of bitterness" toward anyone. We all desire to do what is pleasing to God. It would be an immense gain to our spiritual life if we would resolve not to attempt to pray until we had done all in our power to make peace and harmony between ourselves and any with whom we have quarreled. Until we do this as far as lies in our power, our prayers are just wasted breath. Unkindly feelings toward another hinder God from helping us in the way He desires.

A loving life is an essential condition of believing prayer. God challenges us again, today, to become fit persons to receive His superabundant blessings. Many of us have to decide whether we will choose a bitter, unforgiving spirit, or the tender mercies and lovingkindness of our Lord Jesus Christ. Is it not amazing that any man can halt between two opinions with such a choice in the balance? For bitterness harms the bitter more than anyone else.

"Whensoever ye stand praying, forgive if ye have ought against anyone; that your Father also, who is in heaven, may forgive you" (Mark 11:25). So said the blessed Master. Must we not then either forgive or cease trying to pray? What shall it profit a man if he gain all his time to pretend to pray, if he harbors unlove in his heart to prevent real prayer? How the Devil laughs at us because we do not see this truth!

We have God's word for it that eloquence, knowledge, faith, liberality, and even martyrdom profit a man nothing—get hold of it—nothing, unless his heart is filled with love (1 Cor. 13). "Therefore give us love."

(4) Refusal to do our part may hinder God answering our prayers. Love calls forth compassion and service at the sight of sin and suffering, both here and overseas, just as St. Paul's heart was "stirred"—"provoked"—within him as he beheld the city full of idols (Acts 17:16). We cannot be sincere when we pray "Thy kingdom come" unless we are

doing what we can to hasten the coming of that kingdom by our gifts, our prayers, and our service.

We cannot be quite sincere in praying for the conversion of the ungodly unless we are willing to speak a word or write a letter or make some attempt to bring him under the influence of the Gospel. Before one of Moody's great missions, he was present at a meeting for prayer asking for God's blessing. Several wealthy men were there. One began to pray that God would send sufficient funds to defray the expenses. Moody at once stopped him. "We need not trouble God about that," he said quietly, "we are able to answer that prayer!"

(5) Praying only in secret may be a hindrance. Children of a family should not always meet their father separately. It is remarkable how often our Lord refers to united prayer— "agreed" prayer. "When we pray, say Our Father." "If two of you shall agree on earth as touching anything they shall ask, it shall be done for them. . . . For where two or three are gathered together in My name, there am I in the midst of them" (Matt. 18:19–20).

We feel sure that the weakness in the spiritual life of many churches is to be traced to an inefficient prayer meeting or the absence of meetings for prayer. Daily matins and evensong, even when reverent and without the unseemly haste that is so often associated with them, cannot take the place of less formal gatherings for prayer, in which everyone may take part. Can we not make the weekly prayer meeting a live thing and a living force?

(6) Praise is as important as prayer. We must enter into His gates with thanksgiving and into His courts with praise and give thanks unto Him and bless His name (Ps. 100:4). At one time in his life Praying Hyde was led to ask for four souls a day to be brought into the fold by his ministry. If on any day the number fell short of this, there would be such a weight on his heart that it was positively painful, and he could neither eat nor sleep. Then in prayer he would ask the Lord to show him what was the obstacle in himself. He invariably found that it was the want of praise in his life. He would confess his sinfulness and pray for a spirit of praise.

He said that as he praised God seeking souls would come to him. We do not imply that we, too, should limit God to definite numbers or ways of working, but we do cry, "Rejoice! Praise God with heart and mind and soul."

It is not by accident that we are so often bidden to "rejoice in the Lord." God does not want miserable children, and none of His children has cause for misery. St. Paul, the most persecuted of men, was a man of song. Hymns of praise came from his lips in prison and out of prison. Day and night he praised His Savior. The very order of his exhortations is significant. "Rejoice evermore; pray without ceasing; in everything give thanks: for this is the will of God in Christ Jesus to you" (1 Thess. 5:16–18).

The will of God. Get that thought into your mind. It is not an optional thing.

REJOICE: PRAY: GIVE THANKS

That is the order, according to the will of God, for you and for me. Nothing so pleases God as our praises, and nothing so blesses the man who prays as the praises he offers! "Delight thyself also in the Lord; and he shall give thee the petitions of thine heart" (Ps. 37:4 RV marg.).

A missionary who had received very bad news from home, was utterly cast down. Prayer availed nothing to relieve the darkness of his soul. He went to see another missionary, no doubt seeking comfort. There on the wall was a motto-card: "Try Thanksgiving!" He did, and in a moment every shadow was gone, never to return.

Do we praise enough to get our prayers answered? If we truly trust Him, we shall always praise Him. For

> God nothing does nor suffers to be done
> But thou would'st do thyself
> Could'st thou but see
> The end of all events as well as He.

One who once overheard Luther praying said, "Gracious God! What spirit and what faith is there in his expressions! He petitions God with as much reverence as if he were in the Divine presence, and yet with as firm a hope and confidence as he would address a father or a friend." That child of God seemed quite unconscious that "hindrances to prayer" existed!

After all that has been said, we see that everything can be summed up under one head. All hindrance to prayer arises from ignorance of the teaching of God's Holy Word on the life of holiness He has planned for all His children or from an unwillingness to consecrate ourselves fully to Him.

When we can truthfully say to our Father, "All that I am and have is thine," then He can say to us, "All that is mine is thine."

Chapter 12

Who May Pray?

It is only two centuries ago that six undergraduates were expelled from the University of Oxford solely because they met together in each other's rooms for extempore prayer! Whereupon George Whitefield wrote to the Vice-Chancellor, "It is to be hoped that, as some have been expelled for extempore praying, we shall hear of some few others of a contrary stamp being expelled for extempore swearing." Today, thank God, no person in our land is hindered by his fellow citizens from praying. Any person may pray, but has every person a right to pray? Does God listen to anyone?

Who may pray? Is it the privilege—the right—of all people? Not everyone can claim the right to approach the King of our realm. But there are certain persons and bodies of people who have the privilege of immediate access to our sovereign. The Prime Minister has that privilege. The ancient Corporation of the City of London can at anytime lay its petition at the feet of the King. The ambassador of a foreign power may do the same. He has only to present himself at the gate palace of the Kings, and no power can stand between him and the monarch. He can go at once into the royal presence and present his request. But none of these has such ease of access and such loving welcome as the King's own son.

But there is the King of kings, the God and Father of us all. Who may go to Him? Who may exercise this privilege—

yes, this power—with God? We are told—and there is much truth in the remark—that in the most skeptical man or generation prayer is always underneath the surface, waiting. Has it the right to come forth at any time? In some religions it has to wait. Of all the millions in India living in the bondage of Hinduism, none may pray except the Brahmins! A millionaire merchant of any other caste must perforce get a Brahmin (often a mere boy at school) to say his prayers for him.

The Mohammedan cannot pray unless he has learned a few phrases in Arabic, for his "god" only hears prayers offered in what they believe to be the holy language. Praise be to God, no such restrictions of caste or language stand between us and our God. Can any person, therefore, pray?

Yes, you reply, anyone. But the Bible does not say so. Only a child of God can truly pray to God. Only a son can enter into His presence. It is gloriously true that anyone can cry to Him for help, for pardon and mercy. But that is scarcely prayer. Prayer is much more than that. Prayer is going into "the secret place of the Most High," and abiding under the shadow of the Almighty (Ps. 91:1). Prayer is a making known to God our wants and desires, and holding out the hand of faith to take His gifts. Prayer is the result of the Holy Spirit dwelling within us. It is communion with God. Now, there can scarcely be communion between a king and a rebel. What communion hath light and darkness (2 Cor. 6:14)? In ourselves we have no right to pray. We have access to God only through the Lord Jesus Christ (Eph. 3:18; 2:12).

Prayer is much more than the cry of a drowning man, sinking in the whirlpool of sin: "Lord, save me! I am lost! I am undone! Redeem me! Save me!" Anyone can do this, and that is a petition that is never unanswered, and one, if sincere, to which the answer is never delayed. For "man cannot be God's outlaw if he would." But that is not prayer in the Bible sense. Even the lions, roaring after their prey, seek their meat from God; but that is not prayer.

We know that our Lord said, "Everyone that asketh receiveth" (Matt. 7:8). He did say so, but to whom? He was speaking to His disciples (Matt. 5:1–2). Yes, prayer is communion with God: the "home-life" of the soul, as one describes it. And I much question whether there can be any communion with Him unless the Holy Spirit dwells in the heart, and we have "received" the Son, and so have the right to be called "children of God" (John 1:12).

Prayer is the privilege of a child. Children of God alone can claim from the heavenly Father the things that He hath prepared for them that love Him. Our Lord told us that in prayer we should call God "our Father." Surely only children can use that word? St. Paul says that it is "because ye are sons, God sent forth the Spirit of His Son into our hearts, crying, 'Abba, Father'" (Gal. 4:6). Is this what was in God's mind when, in dealing with Job's "comforters," He said, "My servant Job shall pray for you; for him will I accept" (Job 42:8)? It looked as if they would not have been "accepted" in the matter of prayer. But as soon as one becomes a "son of God" he must enter the school of prayer. "Behold, he prayeth," said our Lord of a man as soon as he was converted. Yet that man had "said" prayers all his life (Acts 9:11). Converted people not only may pray, but must pray, each person for himself, and of course, for others. But unless and until we can truthfully call God "Father," we have no claim to be treated as children, as "sons," "heirs of God and joint heirs with Christ"—no claim at all. Do you say this is hard? Nay, surely it is natural. Has a "child" no privileges?

But do not misunderstand me. This does not shut any person out of the kingdom of heaven. Anyone, anywhere, can cry, 'God be merciful to me, a sinner!" Any person who is outside the fold of Christ, outside the family of God, however bad he may be or however good he thinks he is, can this very moment become a child of God, even as he reads these words. One look to Christ in faith is sufficient: "Look and live." God did not even say "see"; He says just look! Turn your face to God.

How do those Galatian Christians become "sons of God"? By faith in Christ. "For ye are all sons of God through faith in Christ Jesus" (Gal. 3:26). Christ will make any person a child of God by adoption and grace the moment he or she turns to Him in true repentance and faith. But we have no rightful claim even upon God's providence unless we are His children. We cannot say with any confidence or certainty, "I shall not want," unless we can say, with confidence and certainty, "The Lord is my Shepherd."

A child, however, has a right to his father's care and love and protection and provision. Now, a child can only enter a family by being born into it. We become children of God by being "born again," "born from above" (John 3:3, 5). That is, by believing on the Lord Jesus Christ (John 3:16).

Having said all this as a warning, and perhaps as an explanation why some people find prayer an utter failure, we hasten to add that God often hears and answers prayer even from those who have no legal right to pray, from those who are not His "children," and may even deny that He exists! The Gospels tell us of not a few unbelievers who came to Christ for healing; and He never sent one away without the coveted blessing. Never. They came as "beggars," not as "children." And even if "the children must first be fed," these others received the crumbs (yea, and more than crumbs) that were freely given.

So today God often hears the cry of unbelievers for temporal mercies. One case well known to the writer may be given as an illustration. My friend told me that he had been an atheist many years. While an infidel, he had been singing for forty years in a church choir because he was fond of music. His aged father became seriously ill two or three years ago and lay in great pain. The doctors were helpless to relieve the sufferer. In his distress for his father, the infidel choirman fell on his knees and cried "O God, if there is a God, show Thy power by taking away my father's pain!" God heard the man's piteous cry and removed the pain immediately. The "atheist" praised God and hurried off to his vicar to find out the way of salvation! Today he is working for his newly found Savior. Yes, God is greater than His promises and is more willing to hear than we are to pray.

Perhaps the most striking of all "prayers" from the lips of unbelievers is that recorded of Caroline Fry, the author of

Christ Our Example. Although possessed of beauty, wealth, position, and friends, she found that none of them satisfied her, and at length, in her utter misery, she sought God. Yet her first utterance to Him was an expression of open rebellion to and hatred of Him! Listen to it; it is not the prayer of a "child":

"O God, if Thou art a God: I do not love Thee; I do not want Thee; I do not believe there is any happiness in Thee: but I am miserable as I am. Give me what I do not seek; give me what I do not want. If Thou canst, make me happy. I am miserable as I am. I am tired of this world; if there is anything better, give it me."

What a "prayer"! Yet God heard and answered. He forgave the wanderer and made her radiantly happy and gloriously fruitful in His service.

> In even savage bosoms
> There are longings, strivings, yearnings
> For the good they comprehend not.
> And their feeble hands and helpless,
> Groping blindly in the darkness,
> Touch God's right hand in the darkness,
> And are lifted up and strengthened.

Shall we then alter our question a little and ask, "Who has a right to pray?" Only children of God in whom the Holy Spirit dwells. But, even so, we must remember that no person can come unashamed and with confidence to his or her Father in heaven unless that person is living as a child of God should live. We cannot expect a father to lavish his favors upon erring children. Only a faithful and sanctified son or daughter can pray with the Spirit and pray with the understanding also (1 Cor. 14:15).

But if we are sons of God, nothing but sin can hinder our prayers. We, His children, have the right of access to God at any time, in any place. And He understands any form of prayer. We may have a wonderful gift of speech pouring itself out in a torrent of thanksgiving, petition, and praise like St. Paul; or we may have the quiet, deep, loverlike communion of a St. John. The brilliant scholar like John

Wesley and the humble cobbler like William Carey are alike welcome at the throne of grace. Influence at the court of heaven depends not upon birth or brilliancy or achievement, but upon humble and utter dependence upon the Son of the King.

Moody attributed his marvelous success to the prayers of an obscure and almost unknown invalid woman! And truly the invalid saints of England could bring about a speedy revival by their prayers. Oh, that all the "shut-ins" would speak out!

Do we not make a mistake in supposing that some people have a "gift" of prayer? A brilliant Cambridge undergraduate asked me if the life of prayer was not a gift, and one that very few possessed. He suggested that, just as not everyone was musical, so not everyone is expected to be prayerful! George Müller was exceptional not because he had a gift of prayer but because he prayed. Those who cannot "speak well," as God declared Aaron could, may labor in secret by intercession with those that speak the word. We must have great faith if we are to have great power with God in prayer, although God is very gracious and often goes beyond our faith.

Henry Martyn was a man of prayer, yet his faith was not equal to his prayers. He once declared that he "would as soon expect to see a man rise from the dead as to see a "Brahmin converted to Christ." Would St. James say, "Let not that man think he shall receive anything of the Lord" (James 1:7)? Now, Henry Martyn died without seeing one Brahmin accepting Christ as his Savior. He used to retire, day by day, to a deserted pagoda for prayer. Yet he had not faith for the conversion of a Brahmin. A few months back there knelt in that very pagoda Brahmins and Mohammedans from all parts of India, Burma, and Ceylon, who were now fellow Christians. Others had prayed with greater faith than Henry Martyn.

Who may pray? We may. But do we? Does our Lord look at us with even more pathos and tenderness than when He first uttered the words and say, "Hitherto ye have asked nothing in My name? Ask, and ye shall receive, that your joy may be full" (John 16:24). If the dear Master was dependent on prayer to make His work a power, how much more are we? He sometimes prayed with "strong crying and tears" (Heb. 5:7). Do we? Have we ever shed a prayerful tear? Well might we cry, "Quicken us, and we will call upon Thy name" (Ps. 80:18).

St. Paul's exhortation to Timothy may well be made to us all: "Stir up the gift of God which is in thee" (2 Tim. 1:6). For the Holy Spirit is prayer's great Helper. We are incapable of ourselves to translate our real needs into prayer. The Holy Spirit does this for us. We cannot ask as we ought. The Holy Spirit does this for us. It is possible for unaided man to ask what is for our ill. The Holy Spirit can check this. No weak or trembling hand dare put in motion any mighty force. Can I—dare I—move the Hand that moves the universe? No! Unless the Holy Spirit has control of me.

Yes, we need Divine help for prayer, and we have it! How the whole Trinity delights in prayer! God the Father listens; the Holy Spirit dictates; the eternal Son presents the petition and intercedes. And so the answer comes down.

Believe me, prayer is our highest privilege, our gravest responsibility, and the greatest power God has put into our hands. Prayer, real prayer, is the noblest, the sublimest, the most stupendous act that any creature of God can perform.

It is, as Coleridge declared, the very highest energy of which human nature is capable. To pray with all your heart and strength—that is the last, the greatest achievement of the Christian's warfare on earth.

"LORD, TEACH US TO PRAY!"